A ... y of

Chinua Achebe's

Things Fall Apart

OHIO SHORT HISTORIES OF AFRICA

This series of Ohio Short Histories of Africa is meant for those who are looking for a brief but lively introduction to a wide range of topics in African history, politics, and biography, written by some of the leading experts in their fields.

A Short History of Chinua Achebe's *Things Fall Apart*

Terri Ochiagha

OHIO UNIVERSITY PRESS

ATHENS

Ohio University Press, Athens, Ohio 45701
ohioswallow.com
© 2018 by Ohio University Press

To obtain permission to quote, reprint, or otherwise reproduce or
distribute material from Ohio University Press publications, please
contact our rights and permissions department at
(740) 593-1154 or (740) 593-4536 (fax).

Printed in the United States of America
Ohio University Press books are printed on acid-free paper ⊚ ™

28 27 26 25 24 23 22 21 20 19 18   5 4 3 2 1

Cover design by Joey Hifi

Library of Congress Cataloging-in-Publication Data

Names: Ochiagha, Terri, author.
Title: A short history of Chinua Achebe's Things fall apart / Terri Ochiagha.
Other titles: Ohio short histories of Africa.
Description: Athens, Ohio : Ohio University Press, 2018. | Series: Ohio short
  histories of Africa | Includes bibliographical references and index.
Identifiers: LCCN 2018043018| ISBN 9780821423486 (pb : alk. paper) | ISBN
  9780821446546 (pdf)
Subjects: LCSH: Achebe, Chinua. Things fall apart.
Classification: LCC PR9387.9.A3 T53643 2018 | DDC 823.914--dc23
LC record available at https://lccn.loc.gov/2018043018

This book is dedicated to the memory of my beloved grandfather,

Isidro Plaza Prestel,

who was born on Christmas Eve, 1926,
and passed away on July 16, 2018.

El Yayo was my Rock, my Dream Maker.

To his love and support I owe this book and
all of my life's accomplishments.

He gave me wings to fly, and his example,
wisdom, and love will forever guide me

as I fly higher and higher.

Contents

Illustrations

Acknowledgments

I would like to express my heartfelt gratitude to the following:

The English Department at Brandeis University, where I met Carina Ray, without whose unwavering faith in my ability to write this book I would have never gotten started.

Gill Berchowitz, Director of Ohio University Press, for her encouragement and patience.

My two anonymous readers, without whose suggestions this book would have been much poorer.

Nancy Basmajian, Managing Editor of Ohio University Press, and John Morris, the copyeditor of this book. Their attentive reading and gentle suggestions have not only enriched this book, but have made the revision process a pleasant and edifying undertaking.

The Department of African Studies and Anthropology at the University of Birmingham, where I was an Honorary Research Fellow when I started to work on this book, for providing the bibliographical resources necessary for my research.

The students and colleagues at the History Department of King's College London with whom I discussed the making of this book, for their interest and encouragement, especially my colleague and office mate, Anna Maguire, for her very insightful thoughts on the *Things Fall Apart* Wikipedia ad.

Simon Gikandi and Lyn Innes for inspiring me, and for their enduring support.

Steph Newell and Toby Green, friends and mentors extraordinaire, for setting a priceless example of scholarship, humanity, and resilience.

The convenors of and participants in the Genealogies of Colonial Violence Conference, held at the University of Cambridge in June 2012, where I first presented my ideas on *mbari* poetics, for their enthusiasm.

Professor Herbert Cole, whose extraordinary work on *mbari* has so inspired me, for the excellent suggestions he offered upon reading the draft of this book's first chapter and for permission to reproduce his photographs.

Dr. Emily Hyde, for very kindly responding to my inquiries on the illustrations of *Things Fall Apart*.

Angela Andreani, whose friendship and intellectual companionship mean so much.

My mother, María del Carmen, for her loving support across the telephone lines; my maternal grandparents, *Los Yayos,* for their joyful, unconditional love; my aunt Sagra, always there when I call, and her partner César—I must thank them too for the loving care they have so selflessly bestowed on my grandparents in my absence.

My grandfather passed away right before the co-pyediting stage of the manuscript. I longed for the day he would have held this book in his hands. I pay tribute to him as well as to his life companion, my beloved grandmother, Carmen, who, alongside him has been my shining light, and who is left to carry on without him. May the publication of this book bring her a small measure of comfort. May it be a token of what her and my grandfather's union, and their love for us all, have made possible.

Finally, I want to thank Carlos, who bears the brunt of each research project and this peripatetic life of mine, and whose pride, with each dream fulfilled, makes everything worth the while.

Introduction

The publication of Chinua Achebe's *Things Fall Apart* (1958) was heralded as the inaugural moment of modern African fiction, and the book remains the most widely read African novel of all time. It has been translated into more than sixty languages, has sold over twelve million copies, and is a required text at the primary, secondary, and tertiary educational levels the world over. While *Things Fall Apart* is neither the first African novel to be published in the West nor necessarily the most critically valued, its enduring, larger-than-life iconicity has surpassed even that of its author. It is in this spirit that it is included in the Ohio Short Histories of Africa series.

Set in the early years of the twentieth century, *Things Fall Apart* revolves around Okonkwo, a brave Igbo warrior whose drive and determination lead him to the highest echelon of his clan in the village of Umuofia. Passionately traditional, Okonkwo resists European colonial incursion with all his might. After his denigration at the hands of a British district officer, and determined to defend the integrity of his village, he kills a court messenger. Disappointed with what he perceives as the passivity of his clan, he commits suicide rather than face the white man's rope.

While the novel charts the rise and fall of Okonkwo, it affords vistas into the intricate Igbo communities that constitute precolonial Umuofia and its environs, whose people's lives are governed by a supreme creator, Chukwu, and a pantheon of male and female deities. The ancestors, the living, and the dead cohabit—if not always in uninterrupted harmony—and judicial and political power is vested in a council of elders. While not the land of nightmares purported in colonial discourse, precolonial Igboland in *Things Fall Apart* is far from idyllic, and the villagers react to the colonial onslaught in a variety of ways. Amidst detentions, evangelization, court cases, and punitive expeditions, the villagers find ways to survive in the new, perilous order. According to Simon Gikandi, one of the most prominent scholars of *Things Fall Apart*, it is precisely the blurred dualities that form the thematic core of *Things Fall Apart* (tradition/modernity, Igbo/European, masculinity/femininity, orality/writing) that are the source of the novel's narrative power.[1] But the overarching theme of *Things Fall Apart* is the ideological sway of narrative. Crucially, the novel is placed within an indigenous frame of reference. The omniscient narrator is immersed in the ways—cultural and linguistic—of the clan, and retains a degree of opacity that asserts the unknowability of Igbo culture. The discursive and perspectival shift that occurs in the book's concluding paragraphs places the spotlight on colonial discourse and its makings—the projected quasi-omniscience of colonial anthropology, and the gullibility on which the perpetuation of colonial discourse is premised, exposing the ideological burdens of language in stark, resonant ways. What Achebe does is to reflect the results of power over narrative and the power of narrative to redress.

Things Fall Apart was neither the first African novel to dwell on colonial violence, to reflect indigenous realities amidst colonial flux, nor the first to capture the cadences of indigenous languages and literary—albeit nonwritten—forms. Its uniqueness resides in the highly conceptual way in which Achebe impresses all these traits in his novel—an aesthetic and intellectual sophistication that is beholden to his rarefied cultural and educational encounters.

When the novel was published on June 17, 1958, by William Heinemann, London, Achebe was only twenty-eight years old. Its publication brought in its wake unprecedented international attention for the author, a literary explosion in Nigeria, and the creation of Heinemann's African Writers Series. Beyond the originality of its view of cultural nationalism and postcolonial contestation, the outstanding aesthetic qualities of *Things Fall Apart*—including "the epistemological and textual about-turn"[2] of its denouement and the deft transposition of Igbo aesthetics, orature, language, and worldview into the novelistic form—captured the attention of the Western critical establishment, leading to the novel's enthronement in the world republic of letters. The novel's stylistic directness and its canonical status have led to its enduring curricular presence, thereby cementing the text in popular consciousness.

While the novel's literary merits and political impact have been well rehearsed in Africanist and postcolonial scholarly circles, nonspecialist readers of the novel remain largely unaware of the circumstances that produced it. Despite the critical attention, an updated, comprehensive, yet short and accessible *history* of the novel remained to be written. This is what I have attempted here.

This short history is not a work of literary criticism, even if it draws, in great part, on the tools and intellectual production of the discipline. It both explores and moves beyond the text's better-known contexts and thematic preoccupations, to engage with a range of work, much of it published in the aftermath of the novel's fiftieth anniversary, on questions relating to aesthetics, pedagogy, translation, textual materiality, and cultural adaptation and appropriation. It engages with this new and exciting scholarship to ask further questions and provide fresh insights into the story of *Things Fall Apart* as a milestone, addressing questions of canonicity, influence, and textual mediation.

The first five chapters of this work follow a chronological structure, which shifts to a thematic approach in chapters 6–10. The first part traces the literary, artistic, and political synergies behind *Things Fall Apart.*

Chapter 1 is devoted to Achebe's early fascination with "the world of stories," including religious literature, Igbo orality, and, crucially, the precolonial Igbo art form *mbari*. This is a complex aesthetic practice that merges metaphor, symbolism, and allusion in its sculptural representations of colonial rule, and one of the first vehicles through which the Igbo of the Owerri region sought to negotiate, historicize, and alleviate the shock of the colonial encounter. Focusing on the author's "mbari poetics" adds nuance to the novel's representations of colonial violence while situating the novel itself as a modern mbari house of sorts, and it provides yet another entry point for readers of *Things Fall Apart*, as well as *Arrow of God*. The second chapter discusses some aspects of Achebe's education at Government College, Umuahia, but focuses more intently on his later encounters with the literature of empire at University College, Ibadan. It shows how some of his early writing anticipated the formal aspects and thematic preoccupations of *Things Fall Apart*. Chapter 3 addresses Achebe's authorial intentions, the process of composition, and his literary networks. It also traces the manuscript's journey from submission to publication and its postpublication trajectory.

The book's second part revolves around questions of influence and impact. Chapter 4 explores the novel's initial impact in Nigeria and abroad, discussing its early reviews and showing how it precipitated a literary revolution in Nigeria. Chapter 5 maps out the dominant critical strands that have arisen in response to the novel, while chapter 6 develops further chapter 4's discussion of Achebe's contemporaries and their works' perceived relationship with *Things Fall Apart*, raising some questions: How did first-generation Nigerian writers engage with *Things Fall Apart*, and to what extent can their colonial-themed novels be dismissed as imitations? In what ways do these textual connections differ from the avowed filiation and affiliation of more contemporary writers? How does one separate questions of influence and affiliation from those of derivativeness and imitation?

Part 3 discusses the life of *Things Fall Apart* beyond academic circles. Chapter 7 focuses on artistic interactions with the novel, including cover images and illustrations by artists Dennis Carabine and Uche Okeke in the 1960s African Writers Series editions. Chapter 8 zooms in on the novel's two film adaptations: Jürgen Pohlad's *Bullfrog in the Sun* (1971) and Adiele Onyedibia and Emma Eleanya's TV series *Things Fall Apart* (1987), as well as further examples of the novel's intertextual presence in other forms of popular culture, including drama, hip-hop, Onitsha Market writing, and advertising. Chapter 9 discusses the book's circulation and popularity, examining questions of teaching, translation, and reception and arriving at a prediction of the book's future.

This book is not only a history of the most famous African novel ever published. It is in many ways a tribute. As we pass the sixtieth anniversary of *Things Fall Apart*, the first since the demise of its author, it is a fitting moment to celebrate anew and to ask ourselves where the rain began to beat us . . . and if it ever ceased beating.

PART 1

Turning and Turning
in the Widening Gyre

1

The World of Stories

Chinua Achebe (b. 1930), the son of a Church Missionary Society catechist and teacher father and a convent-educated mother, spent his early years in his hometown of Ogidi, a few miles from Onitsha in southeastern Nigeria. Despite his parents' avowed Christianity, he grew up surrounded by staunch adherents to traditional Igbo religion and culture and found himself navigating, almost from birth, "the dangerous potency" of this particular cultural crossroads, which counterpoised an outward allegiance to the new religion and colonial values espoused by his parents with a powerful attraction to the ancestral ways of life. Achebe was by no means unique in this regard, but he had qualities that set him apart from most other children and that would eventually enable him to make sense of his complex world and its constant state of flux in creative ways. The young Achebe was extraordinarily intelligent, and a great part of his intelligence manifested itself in his ease with language and passion for narrative: "first Igbo, spoken with eloquence by the old men of the village, and later English, which I began to learn at about the age of 8," as he put it.

Books did not abound in Nigerian mission primary schools of the time, but Achebe's father treasured the written word and lived surrounded by books, magazines, documents, and inscribed papers of every description. Apart from the Bible, the family's modest library included an abridged version of Shakespeare's *A Midsummer Night's Dream* and an Igbo adaptation of *The Pilgrim's Progress,* which Achebe devoured, as well as such periodicals as the *West African Churchman's Pamphlet.* As we will see, in just a few years' time, Achebe would encounter an equally instructive mode of indigenous inscription, *mbari* art. But in these very early years, he spent considerable time reading the available books and musing on the many educational posters and advertisements with which his father decorated the walls. At this point, however, he was less taken with the world of literature and print culture than with the orality of his ancestors: "I did not know that I was going to be a writer because I did not really know of the existence of such creatures until fairly late. The folk stories my mother and elder sister told me had the immemorial quality of the sky and the forests and rivers."[1] Christianity and the Western literary tradition seemed to him traceable in time—for wasn't his father one of the earliest Christian converts in Ogidi? But there was much to be admired about the timeless world of his ancestors, and he was instinctively drawn to its oral and artistic expressions.

Achebe dazzled his teachers and fellow pupils at St. Philip's Central School, Ogidi, where his ability to take down dictation earned him the nickname of "dictionary." But apart from reading, writing, and the standard fare for primary schoolchildren, he learned an equally, if not more, important extracurricular lesson, which foreshadowed his future writerly concerns. The anecdote deserves quoting in full:

> On a hot and humid day during the wet season our geography teacher decided to move our entire class outside to the cool shade of a large mango tree. After setting up the blackboard he proceeded to give the class a lesson on the geography of Great Britain. The village "madman" came by, and after standing and listening to the teacher's lesson for a short while, walked up to him, snatched the chalk from his hand, wiped the blackboard, and proceeded to give us an extended lesson on Ogidi, my hometown. Amazingly the teacher let all this take place without incident. Looking back it is instructive, in my estimation, that it was a so-called madman whose "clarity of purpose" first identified the incongruity of our situation: that the pupils would benefit not only from a colonial education but also by instruction about their own history and civilization.[2]

This act of historical reinscription was to stay with Achebe for a long time. But it was not the only colorful—yet profoundly influential—educational experience that he would have in those early years.

In 1942, the young Albert went to live with his brother, John, at Nekede, about four kilometers from the southeastern Nigerian town of Owerri. It was the custom in those days for young men and women to take in one of their younger siblings upon leaving the family home. These live-in charges would keep house as they proceeded with their studies. The move to Nekede would have opened up exciting prospects for Achebe's formal education—a new school, new teaching methods and textbooks, perhaps a better-stocked library. But it so happened that Nekede was, Achebe's own words, "a treasure trove of Igbo culture."[3] It was also a repository of colonial history. At Nekede, Achebe first heard stories about the tyrannical district officer H. M. Douglas and the killing of Dr. Stewart at Mbaise, which led to the Bende-Onitsha Expedition, fictionalized as the pacification of Abame in *Things Fall Apart*. And it was here that Achebe would encounter a singular precolonial art form, which was also a spiritual offering and process, called mbari, which existed only in this small section of Igboland, and which would prove to be of abiding influence.

Mbari consisted of ornate architectural complexes housing clay sculptures, commissioned (through the mediation of a diviner) by and dedicated in a sacrifice to the earth goddess Ala and other powerful local gods. The art form featured a repertoire of images, shaped by rituals and artistic conventions, handed down through generations and innovated upon by emerging *ndioka* (artists).[4] Its functions were spiritually and socially didactic, and in this and in its use of vernacular, grotesque,

28

and mythical images, it is analogous to medieval church sculptures. While it is impossible to situate the origins of mbari, oral accounts confirm that it was already well established in the mid-nineteenth century. The apogee of mbari was in the 1920s and '30s, but it was very much alive at the time of Achebe's residence in Nekede. As the culmination of an act of worship, in fact a sacrifice to atone for a disaster, such as the spilling of blood in warfare, and sometimes as a thanksgiving ritual, mbari complexes—some containing more than a hundred modeled figures—were supposed to be transient. And yet, despite the ravages of time, many mbari houses, some with surrounding "cloisters," lasted long enough to be observed and meticulously studied by art historian Herbert Cole before their precipitous decline during and after the Nigerian Civil War (1967–70).[5] By the 1980s, the art form, as it was originally conceived, was extinct. The late 1970s saw the creation of several government-sponsored concrete mbari houses. However, these revival attempts were neither built by expressly trained local mbari artists nor conceptually or cosmologically indebted to the precolonial originals.

If we look only to the handful of occasions on which Achebe alluded to mbari in his biographical and essayistic output, we might be tempted to think that his engagement with mbari was cursory. The best-known connection is probably his suggestion that its name be given to the network of artists formed in Ibadan around 1961, of which he was a founding member.

Elsewhere, he praised "the sophistication of Igbo phe-nomenological thought" inherent in mbari and ndiokas' understanding of art as a communal process rather than a cultural outcome, and described the ways in which mbari captured the perceived attributes of threatening alien forces—most notoriously colonial Europeans, but also local enemies—and domesticated them to ensure the continued well-being of indigenous society.[6]

Nevertheless, as the literary critic Anthonia Kalu posits, such African works as *Things Fall Apart* are "seen as portraying African culture and traditions rather than emerging from them," resulting in the exclusion of the "use of African thought, rhetoric, etc in the analysis of African literature."[7] Kalu, as well as Herbert Cole, has pointed to the fact that Achebe's indebtedness to mbari is more significant than appears at first sight. This is not only of historiographical importance, but "facilitates a new reading of the African writer's efforts to synthe-size a transitional culture." In what follows, I will take up and extend this argument, discussing this singular art form and its documentations of colonialism while tracing an aesthetic and ideological continuum with Achebe's work.

The gestation of an mbari began when, through signs and dreams, the goddess Ala communicated to her worshippers, through a diviner, her desire to be honored and placated, normally after a disaster in the community. The period from conception to comple-tion could be up to ten years. The creation of an mbari was a sustained, ritualized, and exacting process, kept from the prying eyes of the uninitiated, even though community members knew what was happening inside the mbari-concealing fence. Before it was unveiled to the public, a group of elders surveyed the result. Their criticism could, in some cases, lead to modifications. The completed mbari not only reflected its cosmological motivations and the spiritual regeneration experienced by its creators but was also a cornucopia of life—a veritable stage on which the divine, the sinister, and the mundane danced to a harmonic symphony, a place in which "all the real or latent evils [were] composed artfully within an ordered, compartmentalized, open environment in which they may be apprehended and thus, perhaps, controlled."[8] Imitative semblances of living people were typically not included on the mbari stage; it was believed that doing so amounted to offering the person up as a sacrifice to Ala, with deadly consequences. Still, in keeping with its serious origins, mbari was also meant to educate as well as to elicit mirth and laughter.

Despite the socio-religious thrust and entertainment value of mbari, aesthetic excellence was not a subordinate concern. It is true that its formal merits are intricately entwined with "excellence in concept, purpose, and result," but this was achieved, in great part, through the artists' dedication to producing beautiful, yet visually and conceptually complex, tableaux. Neither were the art form's historical-cum-regenerative qualities of secondary interest. For beyond the presentation of sculptures reflecting historical occurrences, which it did by documenting "a cultural history of conflict resolution particular to its specific location and period of construction,"[9] mbari was "a reiteration of cosmic beginnings, a contemporary image of renewal and regeneration that links the real world with creation, tying man to his supernatural forebears, revitalizing the community by reactualizing sacred history."[10]

However, mbari did not idealize indigenous society. Achebe negates neither traditional religious beliefs nor the veracity of supernatural interventions in the life of his characters. Mbari's didacticism was also connected to the insertion of "detailed symbols of traditional religion . . . brought in to remind the now Christian community of its spiritual roots. Everything here is hardened, figuratively and literally, to provide object lessons, a diorama of the past,"[11] an aim very close to Achebe's proclaimed wish to teach his "readers that their past—with all its imperfections—was not one long night of savagery from which the first Europeans acting on God's behalf delivered them."[12] In the ndioka and Achebe's view, it was imperative to alleviate the psychic wounds of empire.

As Cole explains, the "two strings to the inventive bow of mbari artists" included their transformation of existing imagery from "mythology, stories, proverbs, historical occurrences, and the observable life of the contemporary world"[13] into clay models and "more

32

infrequent, the invention of totally new images"—
the heard about and hoped for.[14] In many ways, what
Achebe presents in *Things Fall Apart* is a kaleidoscopic
yet intertextually traceable tableau of similar local and
historical images, incorporating, in the opening lines, a
reference to Yeats's "The Second Coming" and at the end
an allusion to the fictional work *The Pacification of the
Primitive Tribes of the Lower Niger,* respectively the new
"sculptures" of the Western literary tradition and British colonial discourse.

The novel also maintained, in many ways, a number
of untranslatable mysteries—many of the Igbo words
are not glossed, and the significance of certain episodes
remains somewhat obscure to the non-Igbo reader.
This approach is also beholden to the imagery of mbari
houses, which, while telegraphing "Owerri Igbo culture
in its breadth and depth, in both processes and forms,"
delivers some of its messages "as if in a secret or private
code." Beyond instances of untranslatability, "whimsi-
cal surprises always lurked in the wings" of mbari, an
observation that gives the memorable ending of *Things
Fall Apart* yet more nuance.

Representations of colonial whiteness, a recurrent
feature in mbari, also provide another interesting nexus
between the art form and the novel. There were a wide
variety of images, some reflecting origin myths of the
white man (such as a pith-helmet-clad European emerging from a hole in the ground; see figure 1), or the initial
stages of colonial contact (Europeans being carried in

a hammock, for instance, or historical characters, such as the renowned district commissioners Douglas and Cornell peering from second-floor windows; see figure 2), while others portrayed more recent manifestations of the colonial occupation. The first two types, based on rumor and hearsay—and here the reader of *Things Fall Apart* will be reminded of the first rumors of white presence in the novel—were gradually phased out by the latter images, reflecting innovation and transience. Most, if not all, these representations of colonial whiteness "had an element of caricature," despite the violence they tended to encode. The humor of mbari's colonial imagery, however, could very well borrow the title of Glenda Carpio's book *Laughing Fit to Kill* (2008). It was not concerned with stereotypes and their subversion, but embodied "the power of humor as cathartic release and politically incisive mode of critique with deep pathos"[15] that Carpio describes. It was also *literally* fit to kill, for, as Cole speculates,

> It is possible that the virtually mandatory inclusion of his image also reflects a desire for the psychological control, even the capture, of [the white man's] awesome power. When it first appeared, the imagery may also have related to the analogous desire hypothesized earlier, namely, to rid the Owerri world of a formidable enemy by modeling his "portrait," and thus expecting the angry god to kill him. Today such figures are no more than caricatures or historical and

Figure 1: Legends of the origin of the white man—
Beke ime ala (courtesy of Herbert Cole).

Figure 2: District Commissioners Douglas and
Cornell peering from second-floor windows
(courtesy of Herbert Cole).

legendary recording, but there is no incompatibility between these meanings and the hope for control or even annihilation.[16]

But let us focus on the question of the psychological control of the European's "awesome colonial power" as it applies to *Things Fall Apart*. The power tapped into in this case is discursive—and this does not merely occur by appropriating and subverting the textual forms used to inflict and justify colonial violence, but by turning them on their head by using them to portray and convey the beauty of Igbo language, thought-systems, orature, and art. Kalu sees *Things Fall Apart* "as one of the art pieces displayed at Mbari." But I am persuaded to see *Things Fall Apart* as a modern mbari by itself. Rather than rendering a wholesale translation of its principles and conventions, what Achebe effectively does is distill mbari's secular essence, orienting its psychocultural weapons into effective historicizing and cultural nationalist tools and lessons, and infusing the novel—a Western cultural form—with Igbo orality and a distinctive artistic vision. That Achebe described *Things Fall Apart* as "an act of atonement with my past, the *ritual* return and homage of a prodigal son" (emphasis added), has been well rehearsed in the criticism of his work. But nowhere is the ritual component more evident than in the writer's conceptual engagement with the art form mbari. Like the mbari artists of yore, Achebe stages rituals of psychological redress and taps into the circuits of colonial power, transforming and re-defining language in the process of refiguring colonial violence and its legacy along with vignettes of everyday life, while preserving, even if obliquely, an ephemeral but powerful form of historical documentation.

2

Encounters with the
Colonial Library

In December 1943, after the memorable literary and aesthetic encounters of his childhood, a thirteen-year-old Achebe went to Government College, Umuahia, to further his education. This elite boys' boarding school, a colonial version of the distinguished public schools of England—which were anything but "public" in the popular sense—was widely regarded as the "Eton of the East," and, like its British counterparts, was thus expected to instill the mores and attitudes of intellectual and political leaders. There was a caveat, however. The school's idealization of Englishness and the ensuing attempts to shield its students from indigenous religions, cultures, languages, and anticolonial nationalist influences—which were finding fervid expression at the time—implicitly reinforced the colonial status quo, while leaving students to grapple with the arduous task of integrating their indigenous sense of self with the English gentleman ideal promoted at Umuahia.

This type of upper-class British education may seem less than conducive to the kind of mental emancipation we have come to associate with Achebe, but the Umuahia Government College of the time was nothing short of special. Achebe was clearly in the right place at the right time. And the time was never as right as during the principalship of William Simpson, a Cambridge-educated mathematician, which began in December 1944 and lasted through Achebe's school years. Simpson, as Achebe himself would affirm in 1993, would eventually prepare "the ground for the beginnings of modern African literature."[1] I have examined this chapter of Achebe's life in detail elsewhere,[2] but for the purposes of this book it will be pertinent to recall a few relevant facts. First, despite overarching colonial policies, the vocational motivations, pedagogical backgrounds, and political inclinations of European teachers varied widely, and so did the texts they used, the approaches they favored, and the ideological and historiographical ideas they disseminated in the classroom. This had the result of engendering a literary ambience at Umuahia that was largely absent from other schools of the same status in British Africa: Government College had a very complete library, a rule that encouraged literary pursuits, a magazine culture in which Achebe participated as student writer and editor, and an inclusive historical education that included the study of precolonial African kingdoms and oral history research in neighboring villages. The study of logic focused, to a large extent, on questions relating to discursive manipulation. However, despite these potentially liberating educational factors, Achebe's reading of imperial adventures, such as John Buchan's *Prester John* (1910) and H. Rider Haggard's *King Solomon's Mines* (1885), remained uncritical during his Umuahia school days: "I did not see myself as an African to begin with. I took sides with the white men against the savages. In other words, I went through my first level of schooling thinking I was of the party of the white man in his hair-raising adventures and narrow escapes. The white man was good and reasonable and intelligent and courageous. The savages arrayed against him were sinister and stupid, or at the most, cunning. I hated their guts."[3]

But, as we will see, this education would eventually yield fruits that were of crucial importance to Achebe's literary vision. It is significant that all the lifelong friends Achebe made at Umuahia Government College eventually became creative writers: Chike Momah, Chukwuemeka Ike, and, until his untimely death in the Nigeria-Biafra Civil War, the modernist poet Christopher Okigbo. Few writers have been privileged to have such an immersion in the world of literature at such a young age. And literature was to reign supreme on the next stage of his journey.

In 1948—exactly ten years before the publication of *Things Fall Apart*—Achebe's outstanding success in the Cambridge School Certificate examination secured him a major government scholarship to study medicine at University College, Ibadan. University College had opened its doors in January of that year and operated as a constituent college of the University of London under the principalship of Professor Kenneth Mellanby, with an academic staff consisting mostly of early-career British academics. Mellanby was emphatic that the college was to maintain the same academic standards as its metropolitan counterpart, but certain allowances—which would have been unimaginable at government colleges like Umuahia—were made to reflect the changing times. Anticolonial nationalists, for instance, found a ready platform at University College. And as we will see, African religions were not excluded, but held up to academic scrutiny.

In his first year, Achebe set out to enjoy the university's vast intellectual possibilities. But things went slightly amiss. The problem did not lie in his intellectual capabilities but in the fact that, as he eloquently put it years later, he "was abandoning the realm of stories and they would not let [him] go."[4] Despite the risks and difficulties—he lost his scholarship and the attendant privileges—Achebe decided to start afresh in the arts faculty, enrolling to study English, history, and theology.[5]

In his English courses, Achebe was reunited with many of the writers he had read during his Umuahia school years. He also discovered many others. Four of these "new" writers would significantly shape his creative vision. Two were striking exemplars of the tradition of imperial narratives that Achebe had encountered at Umuahia: Joseph Conrad's *Heart of Darkness* (1899)

41

and Joyce Cary's *Mister Johnson* (1939). The first is an aesthetically outstanding novel, part of the high modernist canon. The latter is not as highly regarded today, but received a degree of acclaim in its time.

The English faculty at University College thought that the inclusion of Irish writers in the literature syllabus was, in light of the colonial situation, interesting, and it was under that rubric that Achebe read *Mister Johnson* for Eric Robinson's class. As the novel was set in northern Nigeria, Robinson thought that the geographical proximity might pique the students' interest. Cary's novel revolves around the rise and fall of Johnson, a Nigerian clerk so caught up in his Anglophilic reveries that he fails to see the stark realities that bring about his tragic end. According to Ben Obumselu, then in Achebe's class (and who eventually became a renowned literary critic), Robinson "was trying to recall old Africa, but Cary had no knowledge of old Africa except what he read."[6] What he ended up recalling was something else altogether. It appears the students had already read *Heart of Darkness,* and the discursive continuities with Conrad's image of Africa were glaringly obvious. The students, unanimous in their distaste for the debased representation of Nigeria that emerged in Cary's novel, lost their colonial blinkers. Achebe, as we have seen, had savored, with great relish, a number of imperial novels and adventures at the Umuahia Government College, and now he had an epiphany: "In the end I began to understand there is such a thing as absolute power over a narrative. Those who can secure this privilege for themselves can arrange stories about others pretty much as they like." He decided that "that the story we had to tell could not be told for us by anyone else no matter how gifted or well intentioned."[7]

Things Fall Apart was his first step toward reclaiming this distorted African story. But to restrict the linkages between Achebe the university student and Achebe the author of *Things Fall Apart* to his readings of Cary and Conrad would be unnecessarily limiting. Around this time another instructor, Alex Rogers, gave a lecture series on Thomas Hardy's *Far from the Madding Crowd.* Alongside A. E. Housman, Hardy would imbue Achebe with an understanding of the tragic structure that would become a hallmark of his first novel and much of his work.[8] There were further inspirations. It was only natural that Achebe, who had always "had an interest in our gods and religious systems,"[9] should be entranced by Geoffrey Parrinder's course on West African religions. It was in the course that he first encountered G. T. Basden's *Niger Ibos* and C. K. Meek's *Law and Authority in a Nigerian Tribe,* both of which *Things Fall Apart* also set out to contest.

Having held prominent roles in Government College's magazine culture, it was predictable that Achebe would resume his interests in editorship and creative writing at Ibadan. Of several pieces that he wrote, two anticipated some of the themes and formal features of *Things Fall Apart.* Both appeared in the *University*

Herald, the "establishment" magazine he edited at the time. The first, "In a Village Church" (1951), as its title indicates, was an amusing vignette of a colonial church service. Apart from recreating rural life, it allowed "glimpses of a community caught in the flux of cultural transformation, when not everyone was responding to the same rhythm of events or even singing to the same tune."[10] The second, an untitled short story that was later published as "Dead Men's Path," written in his last year at university, revolved around a young African headmaster's inflexible insistence on disregarding the ancestral right of the villagers to walk through the school premises on their way to the earth goddess's shrine. In his portrayal of the dignified priest of Ani, Achebe captured the linguistic and rhetorical cadences of Igbo speech and the integrity of ancestral religions and customs. The denouement, in which a white inspector of education writes a critical report on the conflict between the village and the headmaster, is prescient of the conclusion of *Things Fall Apart,* parodying and highlighting the reductionist nature of colonial discourse. These similarities are not coincidental. By this time, the world of stories had so enveloped Achebe that he had decided to abandon himself to its dictates. The story of *Things Fall Apart* had already began to take form, however vaguely, in his mind.

The Lost Manuscript and Other Harrowing Adventures

Achebe's passion for the world of stories was shocked into political action by his encounter with Cary's novel at University College. In his 2000 essay "The Empire Fights Back," Achebe affirmed,

> What *Mister Johnson* did do for me was not to change
> my course in life and turn me from something else
> into a writer; I was born that way. But it did open
> my eyes to the fact that my home was under attack
> and that my home was not merely a house or a
> town but, more importantly, an awakening story in
> whose ambience my own existence had first begun to
> assemble its fragments into a coherence and meaning;
> the story I had begun to learn consciously the
> moment I descended from the lorry that brought me
> to my father's house in Ogidi, the story that, seventeen
> years later at the university, I still had only a sketchy
> tantalizing knowledge of, and over which even today,
> decades later, I still do not have sufficient mastery, but
> about which I can say one thing: that it is not the same
> story Joyce Cary intended me to have.[1]

For despite his exposure to colonial notions of English cultural and political superiority at Umuahia and Ibadan, Achebe knew—had always known—that the Africa of Conrad and Cary, a mysterious, impenetrable, yet dangerously alluring continent, a metaphysical wasteland populated by debased, dehumanized peoples, bereft of love, industry, intelligence, and compassion, was nothing more than fiction. And yet the fallacy—whether expressed in popular imagery or political tracts, or wondrously couched in the beauty of literary language—had done untold harm. It had been used to justify unspeakable violence against African peoples and, imbibed steadily and uncritically, had resulted in self-demolition: the subversion of the African mind, in disenfranchised colonial mimics, uncritically adhering to the belief that the West was *the* source of light. This was "the task of re-education and regeneration" he felt had to be done.[2]

Despite his first tentative steps as a writer in school and campus publications, it was not until Achebe's graduation from University College that his budding dreams of authorship began to blossom into reality. Hitherto, he had benefited from studying under a number of brilliant and unconventional teachers and the formidable resources of two elite educational institutions. Along the way, he had acquired a wide expanse of knowledge. But it was simply not enough:

> Welch [a professor of religion and vice-principal at
> University College, Ibadan] helped me understand

that that they were not sent there to translate their knowledge to me in a way that would help me channel my creative energies to tell my story of Africa, my story of Nigeria, the story of myself. I learned, if I may put it simply, that my story had to come from within me. Finding that inner creative spark required introspection, deep personal scrutiny, and connection, and this was not something anybody could really teach me.[3]

If he was to write a novel, he thought, he would have to tap many more sources to convey the cultural, cosmological, and sociological complexities of its African setting, its philosophy, cosmogony, and artistic traditions. In the following years, he would channel considerable intellectual energy toward this task, which was an exhaustive exercise in historical consciousness: an attempt to "look back and try and find out where we went wrong, where the rain began to beat us," as he would later say.[4] To imaginatively recuperate the precolonial world of his ancestors and capture the violence of the colonial encounter involved more than portraying Igbo culture in action—it involved, as we saw in chapter 1, infusing the very possibilities of the novel form with an indigenous aesthetic and sensibility to embody an authentically Igbo creative experience. It was indeed an "act of atonement," but also very much the result of the "boon of prophetic vision" resulting from his own tribulations at the crossroads of cultures. It took the form of a personal catharsis and rediscovery offered up, like the mbari artists' sacrifices to Ala, for the common good of society, with the hope that it might "regain belief in itself and put away the complexes of the years of denigration and self-abasement"[5] that followed colonial conquest.

When Achebe, sometime in 1955, finally got around to actually writing, the novel took over every free hour: "it felt like a sentence, an imprisonment of creativity." He wrote mostly at night, to minimize distractions, abandoning himself to its enveloping power: "It was almost like living in a parallel realm. . . . I had in essence discovered the writer's life, one that exists in the world of the pages of his or her story and then seamlessly steps into the realities of everyday life."[6] Writing the novel was also a learning process: "I began to understand and value my traditional Igbo history even more,"[7] and to understand at the same time the importance of linguistic, cultural, and aesthetic dialogue:

> In retrospect, one of my strongest convictions when
> I began to write *Things Fall Apart*, my first book,
> had to do with a sense that the English language and
> the Igbo language had a lot they needed to discuss.
> Whoever would be conducting that conversation
> would have to be fair-minded, so that mutual respect
> would be established. It was also clear to me that if
> you extend this notion it would mean that the subjects
> for discussion would be diverse, that nothing would

be excluded ab initio. You don't decide that certain things will be in and others out. I thought then that Christianity and the Igbo religion must talk again to me, as they had talked to my father. He accepted more or less the Christian version of events and by implication committed me to that position as well. When I was growing up I was just the most extreme Christian you can imagine. My writing began to tone down that position. I didn't put it as crudely as I am doing now, but that is really what it amounted to: that the whole meeting between Europe and Africa must be reconvened.[8]

As head of the talks department of the Nigerian Broadcasting Corporation, his tasks, which included reviewing scripts and preparing them for broadcast, allowed him to hone a "skill for writing realistic dialogue,"[9] which he "gratefully tapped into" during his long writing nights. "The story was telling me how to proceed," Achebe recounted. "This approach insists on the truth of fiction. Not the truth of history, but the truth of fiction."[10]

Despite the fact that two other Nigerians, Amos Tutuola and Cyprian Ekwensi, had published novels in English in the early fifties (*The Palm-Wine Drinkard*, 1952, and *People of the City*, 1954, respectively), Achebe did not look to them for inspiration: "Everybody has his own idea. I mean, Cyprian had developed one style and one kind of writing and I had no intention to imitate or repeat what he had done. Tutuola was a total world of his own too. But that was one different style and approach and everything, and Cyprian was another. I wanted something of my own style."[11]

The novel he was writing became a saga of three generations of Igbo men: a man who resists the colonial pretensions of European missionaries, administrators, and their troupe with all his might; his son, who converts to Christianity and acquires a level of formal education; and his university-educated grandson, who tries to find his place in Nigeria on the eve of independence. While Achebe wrote in isolation, he enjoyed the company of three of his Umuahia school friends around this time, Chike Momah, Chukwuemeka Ike, and Christopher Okigbo, who, like him, would eventually become writers. Literature was one of their most discussed topics. According to Okigbo's biographer, Obi Nwakanma: "They had arguments. These seemed always centred on certain critical assumptions about the new writings from Africa. They were striving to arrive at their own interpretation of the African past and the African personality and what it all meant in the context of the post-colonial nation. Okigbo was one of the few people to see and read the manuscript when Chinua Achebe completed his first novel."[12]

By March 1956, Achebe had virtually completed the first draft, tentatively entitled *Things Fall Apart*. That autumn he traveled to London to attend a course on radio techniques and production at the BBC Staff School in

London. He took the manuscript along. One of the course instructors, Gilbert Phelps, was a novelist. Urged by a fellow Nigerian attendee, Bisi Onabanjo, Achebe decided to show Phelps his manuscript. Phelps did not have high hopes for Achebe's work but "took it away, very politely." But when he finally settled down to read it he was astounded. He frantically tried to locate Achebe, who was on a tour of the Midlands. The latter recalled: "He found out where I was, phoned the hotel and asked me to call him back. When I was given this message, I was completely floored. I said, maybe he doesn't like it. But then why should he call me if he doesn't like it. So maybe he likes it. Anyway, I was very excited. When I got back to London, he said, 'This is wonderful. Do you want me to show it to my publishers?'"[13] Despite the encouraging news, Achebe demurred. It had been re-assuring to elicit such a positive reaction, but he felt that the novel needed more work, and he was "wondering whether to publish it in three parts or divide the work into three separate books." So he took back the manu-script to Nigeria and set about the task of revising it.

By early 1957, he had finished the pertinent revi-sions. The manuscript was still in longhand, and he decided to get it typed. Responding to an advertisement in the *Spectator*, he sent it to a London firm. But despite his meticulousness, he committed the grave oversight of sending his original manuscript. He paid the thirty-two pounds it would cost to produce two copies and never heard back. His inquiries went unanswered. With the sixth week came feelings of overwhelming panic. He approached Phelps, but he was on vacation and could not follow it up until his return. He then decided to tell Angela Beattie, a former BBC talks producer and his immediate superior in the two-person talks department. Fortunately, she was about to return to England on leave, and she offered to find out the fate of the lost manuscript. She was told that the manuscript had been sent to Nigeria, but the staff could not procure a dispatch book to prove it. Her threats were effective. In less than three weeks, Achebe received just one copy out of the two he had paid for, with no apologies. The incident, according to Achebe, is symptomatic of British prejudice against Africans: "The British don't normally behave like that. . . . But something from Africa was treated differently."[14] Nevertheless, he felt immensely relieved. He believed that the misplacement had been willful: "These people did not want to return it to me and had no intention of doing so."[15] The disappearance of the manuscript would have been catastrophic: "I look back now at those events and state categorically that had the manuscript been lost I most certainly would have been irreversibly discouraged from continuing my writing career," and if he had gone on to rewrite it, "it would have been a different book."[16]

The typescript retrieved, Achebe sent it to Phelps, who took it upon himself to help look for an interested publisher. There were several instant rejections. As he recalled, "some [publishers] did not even bother to read it, jaundiced by their impression that a book with an African backdrop had no 'marketability.' Some of the readers found the very concept of an African novel amusing."[17] Phelps then sent James Michie, his editor at William Heinemann, a whole-page report on the novel, presenting it as "a very exciting discovery . . . difficult to put down."[18] Initial reactions at the publishing house were somewhat circumspect: "The normal fiction reader read it and did a long report but the firm was still hesitating whether to accept it. Would anyone possibly buy a novel by an African? There are no precedents."[19] They decided to seek specialist opinion. Someone suggested Donald Macrae, a professor at the London School of Economics, who had traveled extensively in Africa. His report affirmed that Achebe's novel was "the best first novel since the war." This sealed the novel's fate; despite what a Heinemann editor, Moira Lynd, described as a "slight shortage of commas and a few tiny slips," the novel was published in hardback, without any revisions, on June 17, 1958, with a two-thousand-copy print run. Despite their optimism for the novel's prospects, neither the reviewers, editors, nor Achebe, then twenty-eight years old, himself knew that on that precise day, history was made.

PART 2

The Blood-Dimmed Tide Is Loosed

4

First Impressions

Despite the complex factors that set *Things Fall Apart* in motion, it was, in effect, the culmination of a childhood passion, nurtured in Ogidi and Nekede, havens of Igbo culture, and shaped and chiseled in the most prestigious of Nigeria's British educational institutions. Receiving his copy of the novel was an unforgettable moment for Achebe: "I mustn't forget—I cannot forget the day it arrived, and I was working at the radio and the parcel came from Heinemann, and the excitement."[1] He was a sedate and composed man and took things accordingly. There was no way in which he could have anticipated the novel's reception and influence then or thereafter.

The reception of Amos Tutuola's *The Palm-Wine Drinkard* did not offer clues as to how *Things Fall Apart* would be received, as the two novels were radically different. Despite Western fascination with Tutuola's "tall devilish story"—in Dylan Thomas's words—its reception in Nigeria had been outright hostile; his English and his appropriation of Yoruba folktales were widely derided. Some went so far as to regard him as something of a cultural traitor for pandering—as it seemed to his critics—to noxious Western stereotypes of the African mind.[2] On the other hand, Cyprian Ekwensi, though clearly a popular writer, lacked the literary education and intellectual influences that had driven Achebe's work and shaped his highly sophisticated aesthetic. Reviews of *People of the City* reflected this. But Achebe did not have to wait long. Just three days after the publication of *Things Fall Apart*, the author Philip Stanley Rawson reviewed Achebe's novel in the *Times Literary Supplement,* calling it "a fascinating picture of tribal life among [Achebe's] own people at the end of the nineteenth century." He went on, "his literary method is apparently simple, but a vivid imagination illuminates every page, and his style is a model of clarity." Reviews in the *Observer* and *Time and Tide* were equally glowing, as were commentaries by the novelist Angus Wilson and the critic Walter Allen. Less flattering critiques included David Hassoldt's in the *Saturday Review,* which underscored the novel's anthropological value, and Honor Tracy's pronouncements in her review for the *Listener.* In the snidely titled "Hurray to Mere Anarchy!" she denounced what she interpreted to be Achebe's incongruent and ungrateful dismissal of colonial bounty. Still, unlike in Hassoldt's case, Tracy's sarcasm made room for the admission that Achebe possessed "literary gifts of a high order."

The panorama in Nigeria was curiously different. With the exception of Ulli Beier of the Department of Extra-Mural Studies, who began using the book in his classes, Achebe's erstwhile lecturers at University College, Ibadan, reduced the novel to a "charming" whim. According to Alan Hill, then director at Heinemann Educational Books, the university's undergraduates shared their skepticism,[3] laughing along with Professor Molly Mahood when she joked that there would be "a day when English literature is taught from Chaucer to Achebe." In 1959, the literary magazine *Black Orpheus,* founded by Beier and based in Nigeria, published two excellent reviews by Diana Speed and G. Adali-Mortty, who rhapsodized, "when comments on the content and the style of the book have been exhausted, its intangible beauty remains. Some may call it magic; others the halo, the aroma, the charm, or the unanalyzable quintessence which binds everything together in harmony and unity."[4] That year, *Things Fall Apart* won the Margaret Wrong Memorial Prize, awarded by the trustees of the Margaret Wrong Fund to imaginative work written by an African writer in the English or French languages. The prize was instituted to honor Wrong, a Canadian-born missionary and promoter of African literary and cultural production. The overall early response in its first year of publication can be said to have been quite encouraging, but at this point Achebe's work was yet to be critiqued in the groves of academe. That would come later, with equally variegated, yet debate-provoking results.

The US edition of the book, published by Mc-Dowell and Obolensky in 1959, inadvertently left out

the excerpted lines from Yeats's "The Second Coming,"
but by Achebe's reckoning, it "seemed to 'take over' the
U.K. edition. . . . The Heinemann people seemed to me
very quiet about the book. They were actually thinking
of ending the title after the first print run of 2,000."[5]
Soon after its US publication, reviews of *Things Fall
Apart* began to appear in prominent papers. Apart from
commenting on its portrayal of "primitive society from
the inside," Selden Rodman, in his *New York Times* review of February 22, 1959, called Achebe "too good a
writer," whose real achievement was "his ability to see
the strengths and the weaknesses of his characters with
a true novelist's compassion." The *Washington Post* review by Vivian Yudkin traced the "parallel between
Okonkwo in his nineteenth century Nigerian clan governed by gods and ritualism, and twentieth century man
in a mood-ridden world." As in the United Kingdom,
such reviewers as R. C. Heally, writing in the *New York
Tribune*, stressed its strengths as an anthropological
document rather than as a novel.[6]

If most of the staff of University College in the
late 1950s scoffed at the idea that there was literary
and political merit in Achebe's undertaking, the grad-
uates of his generation saw his feat as nothing short
of phenomenal. In previous chapters, we have seen
how Government College Umuahia and University
College, Ibadan, abetted student literary production.
Many future Nigerian writers tried their hands at
writing—for private pleasure and for publication in

campus periodicals—during and beyond their college years. Their writings might have been, in most cases, Western in inspiration. But there is evidence that some of these youthful writers had begun to revalorize the precolonial past before the publication of *Things Fall Apart*.[7] Still, for all these potential authors, the publication of *Things Fall Apart* was nothing short of seismic. It unleashed an energy that had to a great extent lain dormant—the urge to undo the silencing of the African voice, tapping the vast reserves of ancestral knowledge shunned or rendered invisible during the years of cultural exile. As fellow Ibadan alumnus John Munonye poignantly put it, "The dawn! The dawn came. *Things Fall Apart* was a very good influence. It told us that this type of thing is possible—and by a product of Ibadan, and somebody you know very well. Hey, why not? See what I mean?"[8]

As we have seen, Achebe's Umuahia schoolmates Chukwuemeka Ike, Chike Momah, and Christopher Okigbo had been particularly close to him when he was writing the novel—the last having been one of the few people privileged to read the unpublished manuscript. Acquainted with Achebe's talents since childhood, they rejoiced at his success and were motivated by his feat, and saw in it one more manifestation of a decades-old pattern, uncannily foretold by one of Achebe's school-teachers: that he would make the rain that would drench his schoolmates. The newer friends Achebe had made at Ibadan might have been taken slightly more by surprise, but they were also gripped by a mimetic impulse. Many of these writers have described their initial reactions to the novel's publication, but Chukwuemeka Ike's reflections are more elucidatory than most: "He showed us the way, projected our culture, not just our customs and tradition but also something involving our language. He showed that there is dignity and beauty in our language and he, being knowledgeable in Igbo language had the ability to move from Igbo to English languages and still retain the idiom. He showcased the beauty of Igbo language in English."[9]

I will discuss Achebe's influence on his contemporaries and other writers in chapter 6. But for now, it is pertinent to turn to the question of Achebe's enthronement as the "father of African fiction" in much later years and the ways in which it conflicts with the history of the novel's beginnings. According to the most prominent critic of his work, Simon Gikandi, "Achebe is the man who invented African literature because he was able to show, in the structure and language of *Things Fall Apart,* that the future of African writing did not lie in simple imitation of European forms but in the fusion of such forms with the oral traditions."[10] The latter part of this quotation is uncontestable. But it would be inaccurate to lay *the beginnings* of modern African literature squarely at Achebe's feet. As Ibrahim Bello-Kano affirms, "the idea of Achebe being the 'father of African fiction' is not a scholarly argument but a romantic and naïve one because it ignores the major contributions of precolonial African authors and a huge corpus of African writing in Arabic, French, Portuguese, and Spanish."[11] Along these lines, Stephanie Newell points out, "the writing of West African literary history has for a long time been affected, if not actually distorted, by the foundational, canonical status of *Things Fall Apart*. Critics have tended to condense the decades *before* Achebe's emergence into an expectant, Achebe-shaped pause."[12] As Newell and such critics as Abiola Irele very well explain, apart from Ekwensi's *People of the City* (1954) and Tutuola's *The Palm-Wine Drinkard* (1952), routinely mentioned when discussing the publication of *Things Fall Apart*, other literary works—and by extension their writers—were diminished by the publicity attending Achebe's feat. These include Sol Plaatje's *Mhudi* (1913), J. E. Casely Hayford's *Ethiopia Unbound: Studies in Race Emancipation* (1911), C. Jordan's *The Wrath of Ancestors* (1940), Gabriel Okara's poem "The Call of the River Nun" (1953), Ferdinand Oyono's *Houseboy* (1956), and Mongo Beti's *The Poor Christ of Bomba* (1956), as well as the many writers— apart from the oft-mentioned Pita Nwana and D. O. Fagunwa—who were writing in indigenous languages before the publication of *Things Fall Apart*. And far below, yet more influential in shaping popular tastes than their intellectual counterparts, were the famous Onitsha Market pamphleteers of Nigeria and writers of popular literature on the continent (interestingly, Cyprian Ekwensi's first novel, *When Love Whispers,* was an

Onitsha Market publication in 1947). Furthermore, as Abiola Irele explains, what is indisputable is that Achebe's "genius came to give to this literature a definitive consecration."[13]

5

Things Fall Apart and Its Critics

In *What Is a Classic: Postcolonial Rewriting and Invention of the Canon,* Ankhi Mukherjee asserts that enduring literature "remains so through critical vigilance, evaluation, and free contestations of its implications and ends."[1] As we saw in the previous chapter, the critical assessment of *Things Fall Apart* began almost from the very moment of its publication. And while these early responses—the good and the bad—were heavily contoured by questions relating to the novel's Africanness, with time it has been possible to trace a number of distinct, sometimes overlapping, and ever-evolving trends in the criticism of Achebe's first novel.

While Igbo orality and the English novel were discernible wellsprings of *Things Fall Apart,* its unique literary and linguistic mélange fascinated and mystified early critics. The first wave of scholarship on *Things Fall Apart,* however, stressed questions of orality, language, representation, and authenticity (here defined as the accurate depiction of Igbo society and culture) over and above other aesthetic and formal considerations. Western critics—including Charles Larson, Austin Shelton,

Bernth Lindfors, and Gerald Moore—and their African counterparts, such as Emmanuel Obiechina and Donatus Nwoga, sought to clarify the text's cultural matrix and found themselves, consciously or unconsciously, becoming cultural mediators of sorts. The overt attention to anthropological detail which characterized some of this early work, however, risked falling into some of the discursive traps of *Things Fall Apart*, which in its denouement parodies colonial ethnography and ethnographic modes of reading.[2]

While the course of criticism of the novel cannot be neatly compartmentalized, scholars in the mid-1960s and '70s increasingly turned their attention to more formal and historiographical questions. In so doing, Abiola Irele, David Carroll, Eldred D. Jones, Eustace Palmer, Margaret Lawrence, G. D. Killam, and A. G. Stock, among others, deployed Western approaches rather than methods rooted in indigenous thought systems. Around this time, a bifurcation between "universalists," stressing character traits and experiences that would resonate with the novel's worldwide readership, and those who underscored *Things Fall Apart*'s cultural specificity became apparent. But the division was tenuous. A significant step forward was the critical trend that David Whittaker and Mpalive-Hangson Msiska have described as "Nationalist Universalist Humanism," originally articulated by critics Abiola Irele and Dan Izebvaye and also evident in the work of Ernest Emenyonu and Michael Echeruo.

These critics recognized the novel's dual locatedness in African traditions and Western literary and critical praxis and demanded rigor in the criticism of African literary works—of which *Things Fall Apart* was the most prominent.

As Salah D. Hassan appositely explains, the 1980s were the decade of *Things Fall Apart*'s hypercanonization, thrusting it from its relatively "minor" canonicity in niche African, Third World, and African studies courses and critical circles onto the worldwide literary stage. This, he explains, was due to the fact that the novel "possessed the qualities of the canonical text but remained on the margins because the author was a colonial subject. Designated by postcolonial criticism as an antithesis to canonical works that represented Africa, like Conrad's *Heart of Darkness*, *Things Fall Apart* disrupted the established tradition, but it also secured its place in the canon."[3] Increasingly, the text's aesthetic qualities overshadowed—or at least drew as much attention as—its cultural intricacies. What the rise and consolidation of postcolonial theory in the 1980s and '90s, genealogically indebted to discourse analysis, signified was a deeper engagement with the psycho-cultural tensions embodied in the formal qualities of *Things Fall Apart*. In many ways, Achebe's own essayistic output from the 1970s onward—including the polemical "An Image of Africa: Racism in Joseph Conrad's *Heart of Darkness*"—abetted this new approach to the study of his work.[4]

But even within the postcolonial camp there was considerable diversity. What the novel's postcolonial critics do agree on is that *Things Fall Apart* can be abstracted neither from the Western literary tradition in which it is rooted nor from the ambivalences attendant on Achebe's dual literary and cultural heritage. As Simon Gikandi explains in his seminal study *Reading Chinua Achebe: Language and Ideology in Fiction* (1991), "a reading of *Things Fall Apart* which fails to relate it to the discourse that shadows it, misses the revolutionary nature of Achebe's text."[5] For Gikandi, Achebe's portrayal of Igbo society is a textual reinvention rather than a faithful representation of reality. His reading of Achebe's work, while attuned to its contexts, focuses on form rather than content—including such questions as Achebe's use of the narrative voice and the collapse of the novel's apparent dualities. Writing almost a decade before Gikandi, another prominent postcolonial critic, Abdul JanMohamed, had also stressed the primacy of the novel's oppositional discourse and the "negative" influence of the "racial romances"—Joyce Cary's in particular—which Achebe seeks to counter, as well as the resulting linguistic and formal syncretism. This quality, JanMohamed posits, transcends the novel's ideological double bind: the fact that "the content creates a longing for a vanished heroic culture, but the linguistic and cultural syntheses with the form of the novel point to future syncretic possibilities."[6] In 1991, C. L. Innes took a step further, examining *Things Fall Apart* comparatively with

Mister Johnson in order to explore Achebe's subversion of Cary's entrenched binary oppositions.

For Marxist critic Biodun Jeyifo, the character of Obierika is the fulcrum on which the novel's metacriticism turns. The character enables Achebe to capture counter-hegemonic cultural views, problematizing the apparent polarities inscribed in the novel.[7] Ato Quayson, in "Realism, Criticism and the Disguises of Both: A Reading of Achebe's *Things Fall Apart*," however, implies that such analyses are overtly reliant on questions of representational fidelity. To grasp the full complexities of *Things Fall Apart*, he affirms, it is crucial to probe its very constructedness, "the symbolic discourses that continually restructure a variety of subtexts: cultural, political, historical and at times even biographical."[8] This extends to the novel's gender politics—the patriarchal order and exclusionary practices that pervade the Igbo world of *Things Fall Apart*—which have in themselves triggered considerable critical response.

Rhonda Cobham, Molara Ogundipe-Leslie, Ifi Amadiume, Chikwenye Ogunyemi, and Andrea Powell Wolfe, among others, have held up Achebe's overvalorization of masculine values and his limited delineation of female characters to scrutiny. One of the key interventions in this regard is Florence Stratton's critique of the silencing of the novel's female characters and Achebe's failure to explore and acknowledge the extant sites of Igbo female political, economic, and spiritual power.[9]

Biodun Jeyifo's attention to the gender imbalances in the novel focuses on the programmative "undertextualization of Okonkwo's mother,"[10] while Gikandi draws attention to the fact that femininity is also marginalized at discursive levels, as "the proverb and the masculine stories have more authority than songs and feminine stories."[11]

In response to the critique of the novel's imbalances and omissions, a number of scholars have dwelt on what Ato Quayson describes as the novel's "alternative centres of signification": the apparent salience of Ekwefi and her daughter Ezinma, which he admits never realizes its full potential. However, as he goes on to explicate, "at the level of symbolic conceptualization, the narrative has hinted at its own patriarchal discourse which it has proceeded to undermine most powerfully when describing the colonial encounter."[12] In a similar vein to Ezinma and Ekwefi, the priestess Chielo, Uzondu's impassioned speech on *Nneka* (mother is supreme), as well as the relationship between the couple Nduhue and Ozoemena, can also be seen as alternative centers of signification. Nwando Achebe sums up her defense of *Things Fall Apart*'s gender representations in resolute terms: "While male activities are emphasized in the novel, the female principle pervades the entire society of Umuofia and administers judgement in events in the community,"[13] and explains Okonkwo's end as "a cautionary narrative about the dangers of excess, of disregarding the female principle."[14]

The debates generated by all the diverse critical stances are less than conclusive. The relatively recent celebrations of the novel's fiftieth anniversary and the seismic impact of its author's passing generated fresh and timely studies of the novel's materiality, readership, relationship with contemporary writing, and overall enduring relevance. *Things Fall Apart,* having catalyzed and invigorated a whole field of writing, remains a fixture in the mindscapes of postcolonial and Africanist scholarship, as well as in those of their ideological detractors, bent on preserving the primacy of the "Great Tradition."

Figure 3: Chinua Achebe and Simon Gikandi take questions from the audience during the fiftieth-anniversary celebrations for *Things Fall Apart* at Senate House, University of London (courtesy of Carlos Del Cerro).

Of Canons, Sons, and Daughters

In chapter 4, we saw that the publication of *Things Fall Apart* inspired many of Achebe's friends and acquaintances to take up the mantle of authorship and strive, as he had done, for international publication.[1] For these authors, the spatial, cultural, and educational proximity with Achebe seemed to herald the possibility of fulfilling nascent or dormant writerly aspirations. The following years were a flurry of literary activity.

It was soon apparent that *Things Fall Apart* had turned its author into a literary trailblazer for aspiring African writers beyond Achebe's immediate network. In 1961, during a visit to Makerere University College in Kampala, Uganda, a young student, James Ngugi— later Ngugi wa Thiong'o—sought Achebe's opinion on "Mugumo," a short story he had written, and received his encouragement. Ama Ata Aidoo recalls the "amazing short time" between the publication of *Things Fall Apart* and the demolition of her belief that "Literature, definitely with the big L, was only produced in England by a group of writers who belonged to some sacred society called The Great Tradition."[2] These were all private encounters with the celebrated author and his first novel. But after the initial spate of reviews, *Things Fall Apart* had its first international outing at the landmark conference of African writers at Makerere University in June 1962. At that conclave, which hosted thirty-nine participants from several African countries, the United States, and the West Indies, Ngugi showed Achebe yet another piece, the manuscript that would become his first novel, *Weep Not, Child,* and which Achebe recommended for publication by Heinemann. In December of that year, Achebe became the first editorial adviser for the newly established African Writers Series, which Alan Hill of Heinemann envisaged as the equivalent of Penguin paperbacks for Africa. *Things Fall Apart* was reissued as the first title in the series. Once Achebe had assumed his editorial role, which entailed assessing potential submissions and providing editorial input, he became conscious of the "good, bad, and indifferent writing that seemed in some miraculous way to have been waiting behind the sluice gates for the trap to be released."[3] While he wanted the series to reflect writing from the entirety of the African continent, he was extremely selective in recommending texts for publication. His reviews, insights, and editorial power added considerably to his influence on a new literary generation. As Ngugi put it, "The fact is that Achebe became synonymous with the Heinemann African Writers Series and African writing as a whole. There's hardly any African writer of my generation who has not been mistaken for

Chinua Achebe. I have had a few such encounters. Every African novel became *Things Fall Apart* and every writer some sort of Chinua Achebe. Even a protestation to the contrary was not always successful."[4]

Things Fall Apart was, therefore, instrumental in many African writers' decisions to pursue a literary career. It also demonstrated the ways in which language could, when infused with indigenous cadences, serve as a vehicle for cultural reassertion in the medium of the novel. But Ngugi's words invite two questions: The first—which most critics implicitly seem to ask—is whether African writers charged with imitating *Things Fall Apart* do indeed protest too much. The second, intimately connected to the first, but which requires a more nuanced response, is, when does inspiration shade into imitation?

While this is a complicated question to answer in the limited space of this chapter, a few useful considerations can be proposed. A number of African writers have been labeled Achebe's "sons/daughters," "followers," and "imitators." But in posing the above questions, I am not referring to such exalted names as Ngugi wa Thiong'o nor such late arrivals as Chimamanda Ngozi Adichie. Rather, I am referring to such Nigerian first-generation writers as Flora Nwapa, Elechi Amadi, Clement Agunwa, Onuorah Nzekwu, John Munonye, Nkem Nwankwo, E. C. C. Uzodinma, and Chukwuemeka Ike. I in no way suggest that all of these writers can be ranked equally— with Achebe or among themselves—nor that all are deserving of critical consideration. Nor do I deny the fact that *some* of these writers might well be considered poorly derivative.[5] The fact remains, however, that the work of some of these writers remains devalued by the tag. What needs to be problematized is the wholesale application of these types of designations, and the way in which not only linguistic choices but more superficial textual aspects, such as settings, themes, and cultural contexts of these authors' first novels, are enlisted when describing them as "son/daughter" or "imitator."

Because some of these novels were published in the immediate aftermath of the publication of *Things Fall Apart,* initial perceptions—mostly contoured by anthropological modes of reading—have endured in scholarly circles. Scholars echoing such appraisals today have failed to engage with the vast and generically diverse output that some of these writers have published from the 1960s onward, most of it locally. It appears that the only way in which emerging writers could avoid being painted with the broad strokes of the "imitator" brush was to undertake a radical departure—on the international publishing stage—from precolonial and colonial settings. As Currey notes, second-generation writers Kole Omotoso, Niyi Osundare, and Femi Osofisan "felt that African literature should be about contemporary social and political reality and must explain Africa to the Africans. They maintained that the first generation of African writers had been too concerned with explaining Africa to Europeans. . . . They were keen to reach the emerging general and popular book trade and they wrote for the experimental theatre."[6] That this became the perceived wisdom is borne out by the editorial correspondence on Amadi's *The Slave,* in which readers Henry Chakava and Labal Erapu declared that "the East African reader will feel quite disappointed that after 200 titles in the AWS, we are taking him back to the period before *Things Fall Apart.*"[7] And so it was that when the second-generation Nigerian writer T. K. Obinkaram Echewa published *The Land's Lord* (1976)—a philosophical novel that explores the relationship between the French missionary Father Anton Higler and his Igbo steward Philip, culminating in the priest's transcendent spiritual epiphany—it "reminded everybody of Achebe, Amadi and Munonye."[8] This did not prevent such critics as Richard Lister, Henry Chakava, and Molara Ogundipe-Leslie from lauding his work, tracing other sources of non-Achebean inspiration, and noting its points of departure from *Things Fall Apart.* Ogundipe-Leslie pointed out that the novel "gives flesh, so to speak, to issues previously sketched in Achebe's novels. . . . It is as if one was in the inner areas of *Things Fall Apart.*"[9]

It is important to note that the application of such designations as Achebe's sons—or daughters—has shifted through time. For writers emerging in the 1960s, to be so labeled was, and remains, a backhanded compliment, signaling lack of originality, imitativeness, and thus inferiority. Today, for a young writer to be so tagged means being seen as similarly gifted as, reminiscent of, and yet *distinct* from Achebe and his *Things Fall Apart.*

Hence, some writers delight in the idea of their filiative indebtedness to Achebe.[10] In recent years, the most resounding case of filiation involves the Nigerian novelist Chimamanda Ngozi Adichie, who recalls her own Achebe-triggered "glorious" awakening in ways reminiscent of her first-generation precursors: "Here were familiar characters who felt true; here was language that captured my two worlds; here was a writer writing not what he felt he should write but what he wanted to write. His work was free of anxiety, wore its own skin effortlessly. It emboldened me, not to find my voice, but to speak in the voice I already had."[11] Apart from the shared cultural substrate, Adichie has also stressed her spatial link with Achebe—she grew up in the same house on the University of Nigeria, Nsukka, campus that Achebe had lived in during his years on the faculty. Like many of Achebe's own generation, she also had the pleasure of having the great storyteller praise and comment on the merits of her work. Hence, when she read Achebe's comments for the back of her novel, which stated, "We do not usually associate wisdom with beginners, but here is a new writer endowed with the gift of ancient storytellers,"[12] she viewed them as "the validation of a writer whose work had validated me." While Adichie's *Purple Hibiscus* (2003) and *Half of a Yellow Sun* (2006) intertextually engage with *Things Fall Apart* to some extent, it is her short story "The Headstrong

Historian" (2008) which bears the closest relationship with Achebe's first novel. Variously described as "a metonym of *Things Fall Apart*,"[13] "a homage to Achebe for breaking ground for an African literature," and "a critique of some of the limitations [related to gender issues] of Achebe's vision,"[14] Adichie's story features a recognizably Achebean early colonial milieu, features nods to Obierika and *The Pacification of the Primitive Tribes of the Lower Niger,* and engages with the question of historical reclamation in distinctively Achebean, if more gender-sensitive, ways.

We do not need to go this far in time, however, to see a female African novelist subversively engage with Achebe's pioneering role. Achebe's contemporary Flora Nwapa redressed his infamous relegation of African womanhood throughout her prolific career. Her first novel, *Efuru* (1966), which Achebe seconded for publication in the African Writers Series, was groundbreaking not only in proffering a female perspective on some of the issues raised in Achebe's novel, but in the ways in which the eponymous protagonist surpassed traditional gender expectations. And yet—despite Achebe's imprint on the careers of these two female writers, Adichie and Nwapa, both of whom he inspired and abetted—their work has been read differentially.

The current revalorization of the "son/daughter" label may well be the result of what Elleke Boehmer has called "the inevitable diffusion and etiolation of [Achebe's] influence in more recent decades."[15] In a

2009 article, she exemplifies this critical shift, announcing that rather than "examine features like language borrowing, generic transfer, and the replication of narrative voice in Achebe's literary 'followers'"—as is the standard approach to declaiming imitative derivation—she proposes to "consider the transmission process from his work to others . . . focusing on the relay and adaptation" of the *ogbanje* and twin motifs. This she does in relation to the work of Adichie, Ben Okri, Diana Evans, and her own novel *Nile Baby* (2008). Her conclusion that in "stamping their work with the signatures of Achebe, yet adapting those signatures even as they do so, these writers declare their complex allegiance to, and affiliation with, Achebe and his now-transnational Igbo tradition"[16] affords them a degree of autonomy from the yardstick of *Things Fall Apart*. It is clear that at least in some of the cases, the first point of contact with the *ogbanje* and twin motifs is clearly Achebe's first novel. But would the same critical experiment—flattering as it is—work with Achebe's 1960s "imitators"? Would doing so not obviate the fact that, like Achebe, these first-generation writers lived and thrived for most of their lives in the same cultural universe that international readers have come to associate with Achebe? Achebe himself asserted as much when he declared,

> I for one always resisted the idea that this is "The Achebe School." Personally, I didn't want a school at all and looking back at that generation and you not

being aware what it was like to grow up in a situation in which you have no literature, in which you do not belong to the stories that are told, a period in which you went to school and passed through school and you did not hear anything about yourself throughout that period—unless you went through that, it will be difficult to understand why there was all this to-do about writing our stories, crafting our style and so on.[17]

It is not late to begin this reappraisal. By so doing we would not be demoting *Things Fall Apart* from its rightful place in African literary history. On the contrary, a well-informed awareness of its "companion" texts, as I prefer to see the novels of many of Achebe's contemporaries, would isolate determinant factors in *Things Fall Apart's* literary transmission, rather than shrouding it in generalities.

PART 3

Spiritus Mundi

Artistic Interactions

In 1957, Chinua Achebe, now a successful broadcaster in his late twenties, was happily surrounded by appreciative friends, colleagues, and well-wishers. By contrast, Achebe, the author figure, was very much alone. This isolation had less to do with his protracted writing sessions in the silence of the night than with the fact that—save for the two good Samaritans who stepped in to save the day, as we saw in chapter 3—Achebe had no literary mentor. Apart from the anxiety he experienced in the months leading to the acceptance of *Things Fall Apart,* this lack of counsel was to have long-lasting repercussions on the book's materiality—its cover and interior illustrations. As Achebe affirmed five decades later, "I didn't have an agent when I began writing, which I can't understand now. . . . I had no clue that I needed that kind of protection."[1]

When Achebe's author copy of *Things Fall Apart* arrived, he was too excited to give any serious consideration to the cover image, by Cecil Bacon, on which he had not been consulted.[2] But after the novelty had worn off, he realized disappointedly that it played on widely held notions of "darkest Africa." Apart from the grotesque masks, mud huts, bush, and banana trees, there was the racially charged depiction of two men: a bending, almost crouching, loincloth-clad African and a straight-standing, Bible-clutching, helmeted white missionary, veritable emblem of cultural and religious authority.[3]

The first UK cover was to remain unchanged until 1962. Interestingly, the cover of the 1959 US edition, which depicted an African mask on a black background and was subtitled "the story of a strong man"—an unnecessarily leading subtitle, as we will see—accorded Okonkwo more respect[4] and was considerably more culturally sensitive, even if the cartoonish font somewhat trivialized Achebe's artistic endeavor.

Considering the politically engaged works the Heinemann African Writers Series was publishing, one would expect its book covers to steer clear of the essentializing traits of the Cecil Bacon illustration. But as Achebe—despite his editorial prominence at the series—would find to his dismay, this would not always be the case. Once again, he was not consulted on the design of the 1962 AWS edition. Still, the cover, designed by Dennis Duerden, was an improvement, even if the combination of a mask, a yam tendril, and a Janus-faced calabash was a trifle exoticizing. The drawings that accompanied the text, created by the Scottish illustrator Dennis Carabine, were a far more objectionable embellishment.[5] Taking his cue from the subtitle of the US edition of the novel, Carabine's illustrations centralized Okonkwo's figure and focused on his fall. But this—considering the far more complex plotline—was far from their greatest flaw. As the two scholars who have written on the AWS illustrations of *Things Fall Apart*—literary critic Emily Hyde and artist and art critic Chika Okeke-Agulu—have both indicated, the illustrations, with their heavily drawn contours, are violent and explicitly referential. As Hyde explains, they are "realist less because of their verisimilitude than because they are so sure of their referents, which range from the structure of tragedy to the fact that Africans wear raffia skirts, beat drums, and live under palm trees."[6] Okonkwo's facial features and expressions are overtly racialized, drawn to appear harsh, inhuman, and ugly. According to Okeke-Agulu, "in presenting portraits of Okonkwo as murderer, wrestler, child abuser, and warmonger as the signal moments in the narrative, Carabine seems to have read *Things Fall Apart* primarily as a biography of an immoral, fatally misguided, and vicious native whose inability to recognize the inexorability of European colonial order constituted his most tragic failing."[7]

That Achebe found Carabine's work distasteful is reflected in the step he took shortly after the publication of the 1962 AWS edition. In a rare intervention—his first and last, as far as the materiality of *Things Fall Apart* was concerned—Achebe requested that the drawings be redone by Uche Okeke, a leading modernist artist and fellow Igbo. Okeke recalled the collaboration thus:

Chinua came, I think from Lagos, with the galley proof of *Things Fall Apart* and said that I was the person that should do this. So I took the book, read it upside down, looked at it. I said, that was it, we have our book. By the time he came back I had finished the drawing about the hero Okonkwo and the rest of it. . . . He came, and I showed him the drawings. He looked at the drawings and the only thing he said was—I quote him—"That is how it should be," and left. That was it. "That was how it should be." So what do I say after that? That is why when somebody asks me how many times I sat with Chinua and we discussed whatever, I tell them we didn't meet. We already knew what we wanted. It is as simple as that.[8]

In commissioning, and approving of, Okeke's illustrations, Achebe, Okeke-Agulu argues, "saw the drawings as the work of a co-traveller, a kindred spirit who had successfully developed a potent and appropriate artistic form that would serve as a vehicle for what Appadurai has called the 'work of imagination in the postcolony.'"[9] Okeke-Agulu goes on to outline the experimental pathways of Uche Okeke's own artistic maturity, which bear interesting parallels with Achebe's own educational trajectory—his early passion for *mbari,* his exposure to the Great English Tradition at Umuahia and Ibadan, and his "ritual return and homage" to indigenous arts and culture. Okeke was educated in the prestigious Nigerian College of Arts, Science and Technology in Zaria. In 1958, he became the leader of the institution's Art

Society, the cradle of the modernist artistic movement in Nigeria. Okeke reeducated himself in the intricacies of Igbo folktales and such artforms as *Uli* body drawings and mural painting, all of which allowed him to forge a distinctive, modernist, yet organically syncretic artistic idiom—just as Achebe had done. The formal result, as Okeke-Agulu explains, was a style of drawing "characterized, first, by organic, gesticulating lines reminiscent of trails left by a dancer in the sand. Secondly, they evoke the crispness and directional certitude that is a hallmark of Uli craftsmanship. Thirdly, they provide just enough essential information about the subject, leaving details to the viewer's imagination."[10] The overall effect of Okeke's four pen-and-ink drawings for *Things Fall Apart*, as Hyde very well explains, "is suggestion, not detailed delineation. They rely heavily on the blank white of the page and on a tangled swirl of lines and forms. At first glance it is difficult to distinguish background from foreground, figure from ground. In their difficulty they seem to be works of modernism in the European tradition: they do not yield themselves up as representations."[11] The ensuing differences are not only differences of value—Okeke's drawings are considered works of art in their own right—nor of worldview—Okeke as an insider expert as opposed to Carabine's colonial allusions. Apart from the fact that the "enigmatic, non-realistic" formal contours of Okeke's drawings mirror and retain the cultural untranslatability of Achebe's text, the stress on Okeke's drawings is on the community, rather than on Okonkwo, which, as Okeke-Agulu explains, is "emphasized by the circular composition he adopts for all but the last drawing, which shows the moment this community confronts the alien destabilizing force embodied by the missionary and the church."[12]

Beyond its formal aspects, Okeke's subject matter is radically different from Carabine's: "Instead of portraying a center that is doomed not to hold, Okeke draws a space of collective action, judgement, and choice. Okeke does not depict the aftermath of the burning of the church: the imprisonment and humiliation of Okonkwo and other village leaders, Okonkwo's killing of the colonial court messenger, or his subsequent suicide. . . . [He] illustrates the space of history itself as communal, a space of decision-making and possibility."[13]

In *Things Fall Apart,* Enoch's abominable unmasking of an *egwugwu* culminates in a formidable act of resistance: the razing of the village church. Apart from capturing this incident in an illustration for the novel, it inspired Okeke to compose a poem, "Early Enochs," which "summarized some of [his concepts] of creativity" on the need for cultural integrity amidst the flux of modernity. He also returned to this episode in a 1965 oil painting entitled *The Conflict (After Achebe).* Of Okeke's reiterative return to this scene, Okeke-Agulu says,

> One way to make sense of this choice is to suppose that although the people of Umuofia lost the war with the colonizers, the one raging instance during which

the community demonstrated its refusal to surrender its freedom without a fight presented to Okeke a model of collective action for a society whose survival is threatened by overwhelming outside forces. . . . In painting this subject, therefore, Okeke memorializes that singular imaginary act of popular resistance and returns it, if only symbolically, to the oral history of the Igbo people, whose complex socio-political organization and practices Achebe had reconstructed through the fictive narrative of *Things Fall Apart*.[14]

The artistic synergy encoded in Achebe's request and Okeke's execution of the drawings was short-lived. In 1976, Heinemann reissued *Things Fall Apart* once more under the African Writers imprint with what David Chioni Moore has aptly called "the most inflammatory of all covers," a George Hallett creation, which he accurately describes as "a photo of a shirtless African man raging with a bloody knife in front of a burning cross." He goes on to assert that such a cover would evoke "the KKK. A burning cross doesn't mean much else in the U.S."[15] As Achebe asserted in response to Moore's comments, cross-burning was and remains alien to Nigeria. But Heinemann's reiterated gaffes are not altogether surprising. As Graham Huggan explains, the marketing approach of the African Writers Series "has often shown symptoms of a controlling imperial gaze. This gaze is evident, not just in patterns (especially early patterns) of selection and editorial intervention, but also in the blatantly exoticist packaging of AWS titles, particularly their covers. As emerges from early assessments of titles earmarked for the Series, a certain style and tone were expected, often conforming to Euro-American preconceptions of 'simplicity,' 'primitivism' and 'authenticity.'"[16]

It took other—not entirely fortunate—covers before Achebe was able to feel that the "book had arrived after a long journey, and has made it to the end."[17] It was the 1992 Everyman's Library edition, published in the year that *Things Fall Apart* was first included in the canon-making *Norton Anthology of World Literature*. This new cover, featuring a stylized, grainy photograph of Achebe, in Analee Heath's words, "is a dramatic change from the cheap, often inflammatory editions of the previous two decades. It seems to represent an anointment, at least in the U.S., of *Things Fall Apart* as world literature." Alongside the fiftieth-anniversary Anchor Books edition by Edel Rodriguez, depicting an upside-down head that relays that the novel "stands the story of the world on its head,"[18] this was Achebe's favorite at the time of his interview with Heath and Moore. The 2009 Norton critical edition had not yet been published at that point. Its cover, appositely adorned with an Igbo maiden mask from the holdings of the River Pitts Museum at the University of Oxford,[19] may be the novel's most fitting cover yet, merging cultural specificity with timeless, universal beauty.

Adaptations, Appropriations, and Mimesis

The stylistic simplicity, pedagogic potential, and universal appeal of *Things Fall Apart* have cut across race and class lines to reach an unimaginable variety of readers around the world. Such widespread fame brings in its wake a variety of cultural expressions, retellings, and adaptations, which attest—and sometimes reaffirm—its iconicity and impact. This chapter aims to distill the factors that shape popular engagement with *Things Fall Apart* in different places and at different times.

The first of the novel's popular iterations was a dramatic radio program aired by the Nigerian Broadcasting Corporation on April 7, 1961, entitled *Okonkwo* and adapted by producer Yemi Lijadu and featuring Wole Soyinka. Not much is known about the play, except that it captured the excitement the novel generated among the country's budding intelligentsia, and brought together the two most influential Anglophone African writers. It took over a decade for *Things Fall Apart* to be adapted to another audiovisual medium. The film *Bullfrog in the Sun* (1972) merged Achebe's primum opus ("presented initially as flashbacks that provide background to the political and economic woes of postcolonial Nigeria")[1] with *No Longer at Ease* and *A Man of the People,* tracing continuities between the socio-political dynamics Achebe explores in his novels and the Nigeria-Biafra Civil War. Written by Fern Mosk, directed by Hansjurgen Pohland, and codirected by Ed Mosk, the film, a Nigerian, German, and North American coproduction, was a thoroughly international venture. It featured Johny Sekka, a Senegalese actor, as both Okonkwo and his grandson Obi, and the Ugandan Princess Elizabeth of Toro as Clara. According to its Nigerian producer, Francis Oladele, the film's pessimistic outlook led to politically motivated disruptions during filming in Nigeria: "Security agents came and sealed up my location, bringing shooting to an abrupt end. On enquiry, I was told that I should not make a film about *Things Fall Apart* because nothing was falling apart in Nigeria. So, I said to myself: if the title is the problem then there is no problem. I consequently changed the title to *Bullfrog in the Sun.*"[2]

Achebe had granted Mosk rights to *Things Fall Apart,* but not to his other two novels, leading to a lawsuit. The completed film was "deemed unacceptable" in Nigeria and "was poorly appreciated" in other African countries.[3] After screenings in Los Angeles and Atlanta, the release of the film in the United States came to a halt. It was shown in a number of eastern television stations and somewhat endured in the Fawcett Crest paperback cover of *Things Fall Apart*, which reflected the film's violent nature and thus could be seen as subverting the complexity of Achebe's novel. A disenchanted Achebe was later to affirm that "Ed Mosk tried to make the film good, but clearly didn't succeed."[4] Over and above the narrative and cinematic inefficacy of the film, the unlawful appropriation of Achebe's two other novels struck a sour note, highlighting, as Carabine's illustrations of Achebe's novel and many of the novel's covers did, that material interactions with a literary work—despite the potential effects on a work's reception—were beyond the control of its author.

In 1977, Ogali A. Ogali, the best-selling and most prominent Onitsha author, most of whose pamphlets dramatized the dangerous allure of modern life in Nigerian cities, wrote a full-length novel entitled *The Juju Priest*. The novel is striking for its colonial theme—by then no longer fashionable among Nigeria's intellectual writers, and of negligible interest for Onitsha pamphleteers. More striking still is its engagement with Achebe's *Things Fall Apart*, from which it borrowed a number of Achebean motifs, including the evil forest and the preaching scene, but most importantly, the subversive use of the ethnographic narrative voice in the exposure of the makings and psychological effects of colonial discourse.[5]

Achebe was at the height of his fame in the mid-1980s,[6] a period that saw two important Nigerian adaptations of *Things Fall Apart*. The first was Bassey

93

Effiong's play of the same name, which was staged by the Anansa Playhouse, Lagos, in November 1985 and subsequently toured the country. The second, an epic production for the Nigerian Television Authority (NTA), which aired in 1986,[7] was a highlight in the history of Nigerian television, and was to become iconic in its own right.

The thirteen-episode series was commissioned by Dr. Walter Ofonagoro, then director general of the NTA. Ofonagoro was a historian of Africa and was convinced of the novel's potential for didactic entertainment. Adiele Onyedibia and Emma Eleanya were assigned the task of writing the script, and the completed series was released in English. Because of the series' duration, it was possible to relay the Igbo cultural manifestations portrayed in Achebe's novel in considerable detail, resulting in minute representations of dances, meetings, wrestling contests, kola-breaking ceremonies, and other customs. Combined with the painstakingly selected settings (*Things Fall Apart* was filmed in various southeastern Nigerian locations), magnificent costuming, and a memorable traditional Igbo soundtrack, the series provided an impressive documentation of Igbo language, landscapes, and culture. The well-known passages of Achebe's novel come alive in this choral production, and—despite the elision of a number of chapters—the full narrative of *Things Fall Apart* made it into the series, in both dialogues and voiceovers. There were a number of amplifications of the original plotline, the most important of which elaborates on the issues surrounding the killing of an Umofia woman by two men from Mbaino, the consequences on some of the affected households of this village, and, most significantly, Okonkwo's last moments before committing suicide.

The NTA *Things Fall Apart* series was a roaring success. Its celebration of traditional culture was a key element, as was its visual sophistication. But beyond these crucial elements, two aspects in particular have endured in collective consciousness: the theme song and the figure of *Ebubedike*, the praise name with which Okonkwo was constantly acclaimed in the series. As Françoise Ugochukwu elaborates in her intricate analysis of the film, the title song

> expanded on the writer's choice of a line from Yeats's poem "The Second Coming." . . . The miniseries borrowed the first two lines from Yeats's poem for the lyrics of its opening music, altering them slightly by replacing the word "world" with the more appropriate "land" and repeating lines one and two. The song also added two additional lines, repeated at the end of each line, written as pendants to Yeats's text:
>
> > Things fall apart and the centre cannot hold;
> > Things fall apart and the centre cannot hold;
> > Mere anarchy is loosed upon the world.
> > We must not fall apart
> > We must not fall apart
> > Lest anarchy be loosed upon our land.

This significant addition to Yeats's poem placed the series in line with Igbo oral genres, characterized by oppositions and repetitions.[8]

One of the most notable features of the NTA *Things Fall Apart* series was the centralization and positive embellishment of Okonkwo's character. In contrast to his much-critiqued misogyny and rashness in the novel, the series' Okonkwo, though quick to anger, is more easily cajoled into conformity and shows a much more considerate and caring side. His praise-name, Ebubedike (literally Glorious Warrior), pervades the music and dialogue—a constant reminder of Okonkwo's might and splendor. Aligned to this renewed image is the revalorization of Unoka's character. As Ugochukwu explains, "in the screen adaptation . . . Unoka is still alive and portrayed as a tender, loving husband and an inspiring father, passionate about music and eager to share this with those around him. Members of his close family [including Okonkwo] who somewhat blame him for his laid-back attitude to work, recognize his musical talent and show some appreciation for it."[9]

This more positive representation of Okonkwo contributed in large measure to enshrining the leading actor, the Nollywood star Pete Edochie, in the collective memory as Okonkwo, and Ebubedike became Edochie's de facto name. As the actor puts it, "when you walk around the entire country, Pete Edochie is known as Okonkwo, Ebubedike, and that name will follow me to the grave. Even Chinua himself calls me Ebubedike."[10] But beyond Okonkwo's reimagined gentleness and Edochie's eloquent portrayal, the actor believes that the audience was taken with Okonkwo because Onyedibia had imagined him "as a concept" rather than as a character. As Edochie expounds, "Okonkwo as an individual represents an ideology. Okonkwo was resisting an incursion into the sacrosanctity of those cultures by the white man, so that rather than stay alive and witness the rape of his own culture, he elected—in honour—to take his own life. . . . That was how we approached it and that was why it succeeded."[11]

As Ugochukwu further explains, Okonkwo's suicide is substantially reframed—thanks to one of the film's additions to Achebe's original story:

> In the scenes preceding Okonkwo's suicide, he
> expresses his frustration, anger, and desperation, as
> he now clearly perceives his people cowering under
> British rule. He asks his friend Obierika, "Is it a crime
> to stand up for this land? Is it a crime to protect my
> people? . . . The white man's ways are not our ways."
> Later, after killing the court messenger, Okonkwo
> returns to his deserted compound and calls his
> ancestors one last time: "Let my cause remain alive!
> Let Umuofia remain alive! Let my people be allowed
> to live their own way!" These added words throw more
> light onto Okonkwo's mindset, reflect his concern for
> his land and culture, and present his death not as the

result of a personal humiliation and defeat, but as the refusal to live and see the Igbos defeated.[12]

While Achebe's novel is a cultural nationalist production in every aspect, its anticolonial dimension is understandably minimized in the series, which, produced for a Nigerian audience, omits the narrative shift at the novel's ending, finishing instead "with a string of flashbacks summarizing key moments of Okonkwo's life—a celebration of him and his courage."[13] As Ugochukwu affirms, " the film version of *Things Fall Apart* did make the novel more popular [and] consolidated Nigerians' views on their colonial history."[14] It also garnered a degree of international interest. Pete Edochie's portrayal of Okonkwo won him international accolades, and as he recalls, the BBC interviewed both him and Achebe upon the release of the film.[15]

In 1997, the Nigerian writer Biyi Bandele adapted *Things Fall Apart* for the stage. The adaptation was directed by Chuck Mike, an American director who had spent many years in Nigeria, choreographed by Chukwuma Okoye, and originally coproduced by the London International Festival of Theatre (LIFT) and the West Yorkshire Playhouse. The play opened on June 12, 1997, at the Royal Court Theatre Upstairs (part of the Ambassadors Theatre) to an enthusiastic reception. It went on an international tour, including the Nigerian cities of Lagos and Abuja. In 2011, Mike reprised the play, and again in 2013 during a short run in memory of Achebe, he discussed the experience of watching the play with the author himself at the McCarter Theatre, Princeton. According to Mike, Achebe's face was inexpressive during the performance, but at the end of the play, he affirmed, "I've seen a few attempts at this work but today I saw what I wrote."[16]

In 1999, the Roots, a band from Philadelphia, released their fourth and most successful album, *Things Fall Apart*, with a shock value that "changed the current of traditional hip-hop."[17] The band had a unique sound, which "wasn't jazz-rap or alternative hip-hop, it wasn't for the streets or the college dorms. It was too precise, too unique for that."[18] According to James Braxton Peterson, "Throughout much of their career, they have produced art as if the challenge has been to raise those expectations to new levels. This is at least partially why the Roots can claim a common plight with the characters of Achebe's classic novel. As musicians they are committed to the roots and traditions of Black Music."[19] The album revolved around the convolutions of the black experience in the United States, featuring fifteen songs—one of which was entitled "Act Won (Things Fall Apart)"—and closing with a poem by Ursula Rocker on violence in an interracial marriage.

Almir "Questlove" Thompson, the drummer and joint frontman of the Roots, explained their inspiration for their album:

> The Chinua Achebe novel of the same name is about a Nigerian man who returns to his village to find

the only constant was change, that Western ways were wiping out the traditions that made his culture distinctive. That resonated with me as an analogy for what had happened to hip-hop: we were part of a music that had, at least early on, been so new, so true to itself, but there had been a corruption from the outside, and what was once there was gone. That was the spatial dimension of the idea, inside threatened by outside, but there was a temporal dimension, too, tradition threatened by newcomers.[20]

To further establish links with Achebe's novel, in the track "100% Dundee," the group's leading MC, Black Thought, alludes to its author:

> Plus the black Thought em-cey, professional-lay
> Push pen to paper like Chinua Achebe
> Thumping, what your assumption
> I lace your function, make it a Black Thought
> production.

According to Richard Dryden, "the shock value of *Things Fall Apart* grew The Roots' reputation for raising public awareness in both their music and on their album covers."[21] The album was issued with five alternative covers, featuring different black-and-white photographs selected by art director Kenny Gravillis, and two of the photographs are curiously resonant with some of the preoccupations behind Achebe's novel. The first, *Woman Running*, shot anonymously in Brooklyn in the 1960s, depicts a young black woman running from a white police officer, her face contorted by fear. Alongside the woman is a black man, running from the policemen with what look to be torn shirtsleeves. While not intentionally, the inclusion of a black-and-white photograph of a bombed church is curiously reminiscent of the Enoch episode that modernist artist Uche Okeke recreated more than once in his engagement with the novel.

The last—and notoriously unsuccessful—attempt from a well-known member of the hip-hop community to appropriate the title of *Things Fall Apart* fell flat on its face. The rapper Curtis James Jackson III, popularly known as 50 Cent, tried to use the title for a film he was producing and acting in. As Sean Michaels reported in the *Guardian,*

> Unfortunately for Fiddy, his film will not keep its original title. After being contacted by Achebe's legal team, 50 Cent allegedly offered $1m to hold on to the title. Achebe, 80, took this as an insult. "The novel with the said title was initially produced in 1958 (that is 17 years before [50] was born)," replied his lawyers, according to Naijan. "[It is] listed as the most-read book in modern African literature, and won't be sold for even £1bn." The film has now been renamed to *All Things Fall Apart.*[22]

But the story of the film's adaptations and spin-offs ends on a far more memorable note. In September 2017, thirty-one years after the NTA *Things Fall Apart* series that made his fame, Pete Edochie returned to the most important role of his career, Okonkwo. This time, Ebubedike appeared in a three-minute promotional film produced by Anakle, entitled *Things Come Together*, to promote Wikipedia in Nigeria. The film, directed by Sam Oyeyele, Blossom Ozurumba, Kayode Yussuf, Eyitayo Alimi, and Olushola Olaniyan, begins in an adult education class in the village of Umuofia. The schoolmaster asks the group of villagers—which crucially includes women among titled men—to tell him about "the most famous adaptation of 'The Second Coming' by William Butler Yeats." Obi-erika,[23] one of the village chiefs (played by Nduka Eya, Ezeudu in the original film), replies, "Mr. Yeats wrote a white man's poem, but a great son of the soil, Chinua Achebe, put it in his book where he told us the story of our great village and our hero seated here." Okonkwo smiles beatifically from the background. The class continues, and Obi-erika brilliantly responds to the schoolmaster's question on polytheism, bursting with cultural pride. The schoolmaster does not "correct" Obi-erika's valorization of indigenous culture, but praises him for his intelligence. After the class, Obi-erika walks with Okonkwo to the village. When the two men finally sit together, Okonkwo asks Obi-erika the source of his broad knowledge. Conspiratorially, Obi-erika retrieves a mobile phone, singing the praises of Wikipedia. The film can be interpreted as an alternative trajectory for Okonkwo's character, and it is significant that *Things Fall Apart* is made to stand for

Figure 4: *Ebubedike* Redivivus: *Things Come Together* (2017) (photo by Wikimedia Foundation CC-BY-SA 4.0).

world knowledge.[24] Also important is the subversion of Yeats's canonicity implied in Obi's response on Achebe's appropriation of the poem's lines in the novel. But beyond critical interpretations, and despite the temporal incongruities, it is possible to suspend belief in this singular return of Ebubedike to Nigerian households, and, thanks to the internet, to the world over. Edochie may now be a venerable elderly man, and a mobile phone may emerge from a chief's wrapper, but the interspersion of English and Igbo in the dialogue, the beauty of the Igbo village, the sunshine, joy, and ancient turns of phrase, and the reiterative enunciation of the praise name Ebubedike are signifiers of *Things Fall Apart*'s enduring relevance.[25]

Things Fall Apart's
Worldwide Readers

What pathways has *Things Fall Apart* followed in its circulation among lay readers? Most citations of the novel stress the impressive number of languages into which it has been translated (sixty at the last reckoning) and its presence as a permanent fixture in history, literature, sociology, anthropology, African studies, literary theory, and political science courses in classrooms around the world. As we saw in chapter 5, critical acclaim is a key step toward literary canonicity. A work's circulation in the world republic of letters, albeit dependent on academic seals of approval, is no less crucial. Teachers, reviewers, translators, public libraries, and publishing houses are key institutions for a work's longevity and public consumption. Articles and book chapters abound on the teaching, translation, and reader reception of *Things Fall Apart*, and it is not difficult to deduce common patterns in the novel's nonscholarly trajectories. These continuities are useful in isolating the factors behind the novel's popularity in some parts of the world, and interrogating its relative obscurity in others.

As we saw in chapter 4, even though *Things Fall Apart* was first published in London and took some months to arrive on African shores, its curricular presence opened vast cultural vistas for colonial students, and subsequently for their postcolonial successors. Since the novel has been replaced by the work of other African writers in secondary school curricula, today's African readers are likely to become acquainted with it elsewhere, either because of its author's fame or after encounters with some of his shorter works, such as his war poetry and children's books. Even though *Things Fall Apart* bears none of the ideological burdens of "postcolonial literature" in African classrooms, the ways in which it captures the integrity of Igbo society before colonial invasion has inspired generations of students and adult readers. African readers of *Things Fall Apart* tend to be captivated by its cultural representations, although for different reasons than their Western counterparts. Kwame Anthony Appiah's affirmation that "for those of us raised largely with texts that barely acknowledged the specificity of our existence, each work that simply placed us before the world we already know ... can provide a moment of self-validation"[1] still holds true today, as present-day rural societies in Africa retain vestiges of the world captured in *Things Fall Apart*. By all accounts, Achebe's wish to teach his readers that "their past—with all its imperfections—was not one long night of savagery from which the first Europeans acting on God's behalf delivered them" will continue to be fulfilled in the foreseeable future.

Many of *Things Fall Apart*'s Western readers may not have read any other work by an African writer, and the novel's potential to overturn preconceptions of the continent and its people and cultures is immense. But it does not always fulfill this potential, as we will see. Most of the available information on the teaching of the novel and its reception has been assembled in the Anglophone Western countries. And as the figures show, *Things Fall Apart* has made its way to almost all corners of the world. On the one hand, one of the novel's selling points is its simplicity and accessibility. On the other, the text's contextual and linguistic unfamiliarity could impair intercultural communication. Judging from available studies, what can we make of this apparent conundrum?

While many African readers' gaze is one of identification—village life, the clash between tradition and modernity, and the characters' patent Africanness being qualities that tend to hold this readership in thrall—the novel's Western readers are prone to an exoticizing gaze. In reflecting on the letters he received from a group of high school readers of *Things Fall Apart* from New York, in which they described their elation at learning "about the customs and superstitions of an African tribe," Achebe rooted such readings in "the desire—one might indeed say the need—in Western psychology to set Africa up as a foil to Europe, as a place of negations at once remote and vaguely familiar, in comparison with which Europe's own state of spiritual grace will be manifest."[2] Whether or not one agrees with this statement, it does underline the way African works tend to be approached with a patent disregard for their literariness.

James Procter analyzes an online discussion of the novel between readers in Kano, Lagos, London, and Glasgow, hosted by the British Council Encompass website. He describes the ways in which Western readers asked questions that positioned Nigerian readers as "native" informants, whereas Nigerian readers "disavow[ed] the ideological, postcolonial narrative of *Things Fall Apart,* by either shrinking it to the personal/psychological, or expanding it in ways that suggest it exceeds, or is always about more than, a cultural conflict between colonizer and colonized, Europe and Africa."[3] These universalist claims, which are "more than merely naïve liberal humanism in this context," are used to "short-circuit attempts by some of the UK-based readers, unconsciously or not, to frame the book in purely ethnographic/sociological terms, or to fix it in a literal, referential manner by insisting on the book's provenance over its status as a mobile cultural artefact." This they do by insisting implicitly on its literariness.[4] Procter's reading of this interaction between African and Western readers is most insightful, as is his engagement with John Guillory's comments on the lack of mutual understanding between lay and professional readers, who fail to "comprehend why their modes of reading do not translate into a wider transformative culture."[5]

To borrow Wahneema Lubiano's phrase, in most cases the Western "audience [is] predisposed, even educated, to read [*Things Fall Apart*] only as ethnography and simple cultural representation of the exotic other."[6] The cultural specificity of the African text is incontestable. And yet the exoticism of its marketing and production necessarily lead to preconceived forms of reading that might actually create specific niches, expectations, and ethical valorizations not necessarily deployed in intracultural acts of reading.[7] What needs to be found is a way of untangling cultural specificity from form. Is the real obstacle to intercultural communication the baggage that comes with the word "African," the stress on the novel's ideological thrust (in and outside the classroom), or the exoticizing materiality in which publishers, translators, book club leaders, and non-academic reviewers couch the book? In other words, is there a way of eliciting more *literary* appreciations? I will take up these questions shortly. For now, suffice it to say that they are somewhat connected to the issues of translational mediation that influence the reception of Achebe outside the anglophone context.

Writing on the differing reactions to Tutuola's *The Palm-Wine Drinkard* and *Things Fall Apart* in France, Ruth Bush posits that a text's established prestige in its language or sphere of origin is not as eminently transferable to other linguistic contexts as one would expect. The prestige of the translator and publisher can endow a literary work with an aura lacking by works translated and published by less renowned outlets. Hence, Achebe's work was sidelined in the "Left Bank heartlands of the world republic of letters" because of the "weak legitimating power of Achebe's translator and publisher [Michel Ligny and Présence Africaine, respectively] within the literary field" in the late 1960s.[8] As Bush shows, the consequences of this kind of literary snobbery on a book's fortunes are anything but negligible, for in the case of Achebe, the "responsibility for 'the rise of the African novel,' which critics place almost wholly on his shoulders, looks less monumental when we consider his location in the francophone literary field and the relationship between these spaces."[9] In 2012, the four editions of the novel in French—the most recent published in 2006—were out of print.

In Spain, the most recent translation of Achebe's novel, published by Random House Mondadori (2010), is still in print, but this has more to do with the fact that it never made much of an impression on the Spanish market. Its translator, Marta Sofía López, asserts that the publisher's sole motivation for acquiring the Spanish-language rights to Achebe's works was his Nobel Prize candidacy, and that—beyond the sociocultural realities that preempt Spanish reader affinity for works on Africa *written by Africans*—the publisher failed to promote the translations adequately, and indiscriminately tampered with the book's introduction, as well as the translation itself, during the copy-editing process.[10] Earlier Spanish translations of the novel remain out of print. While the French and Spanish literary marketplaces are not representative of all the contexts in which Achebe's work has been translated, they do exemplify how in many countries "Achebe [and by extension *Things Fall Apart*] remains a canonical figure in hiatus, suspended between the Anglophone African literary 'world' of which he has been concerned as the 'inventor' and his fleeting presence."[11]

When an African literary work is reviewed in the West, especially in countries with few to no African colonial connections, and in which a consciousness of imperial colonial history is thus not as embedded in the collective psyche, there is always a risk that reviews will, apart from stressing context over text, evince colonialist frames of reference, rehashing stereotypes of African savagery and stressing postcolonial failures. Raoul Granqvist shows this in his study of Swedish reviews of the 1967 translation of *Things Fall Apart,* where, unlike in France and Spain, "Achebe was the first black African writer to be received in Sweden with some acclaim and momentum" upon translation. What needs to be stressed, however, is not how reviews can impact a novel's international possibilities, but how they affect its reading and reception.[12]

A survey of teaching publications on *Things Fall Apart* shows that its use as a set text presents related challenges. While the novel, to quote Bernth Lindfors, "has subtle and profound dimensions that those coming to it for the first time might easily miss,"[13] to emphasize context to the detriment of form, as many teachers of the novel do, can be a serious limitation. And frequently teachers' best intentions can be marred by their own cultural misinterpretations. This tends to be the case in courses in which *Things Fall Apart* is tokenized as an introduction to "a different culture."

The solution is not simply to do away with biographical and cultural contexts but to use them in the exact ways they would be deployed in the study of a Western literary work. Apart from the relatively common strategy of prompting students to read Achebe's novel side by side with its most famous intertexts, *Heart of Darkness* and *Mister Johnson,* several teachers—some of them renowned critics—propose a wide range of solutions. To give just two examples, in 1991, Simon Gikandi reported using his genre course to encourage students to read *Things Fall Apart* as "a particular kind of contemporary novel—one written under the influence of high modernism but still relying on traditional nineteenth century conventions of narration."[14] In a similar line, Lubiano advocated for a pedagogy that "makes visible the artifice and self-willed intentionality of the text as a cultural object" by exploring its repressed form, or rather its narrative structures.[15]

As Achebe affirmed in his essay "Teaching *Things Fall Apart,*" he had "known the book if not more intimately, then at least for a longer period than anybody else around."[16] Still, he never taught his most famous novel. His choice to devote this particular essay to his encounters with a variety of readers—not just students—shows how intimately linked *Things Fall Apart*'s classroom use can be to its dissemination in the world beyond. To reflect on one is to reflect on the other, to recognize the connection between the ivory tower of academia and the mundane world, and the often unacknowledged social responsibility of the literary critic.

Conclusion

Whither *Things Fall Apart*?

"We live in revolutionary and exciting times."

Thus begins Achebe's little-known essay "Continuation and Change in Nigerian Education," written and published in 1979. And while his choice of adjectives responded to very different politico-temporal imperatives, they are applicable today. "Revolutionary because profound changes are taking place all around us every day," he went on. Exciting, I will add, because of the vast wealth of possibilities open to humanity today.

Sixty years have passed since the publication of *Things Fall Apart*. Sixty years of social, racial, and political advances that could have at least yielded "the first fruits of the balance of stories among the world's peoples," as Achebe had arduously desired. And still, as most scholars and teachers of *Things Fall Apart* based at Western educational institutions will agree, there are no great differences between the challenges faced by the novel's first teachers and those we face today. Neither collective consciousness of empire nor the ever-increasing racial diversity in what used to be predominantly white spaces has done much to jettison the vestiges of the colonial discourse and mental colonization that prompted, in part, Achebe's momentous decision to embark on the journey to write this extraordinary novel.

It is tempting indeed to stress *Things Fall Apart*'s contestatory message, to linger on his realist representations, and to get mired in his precolonial Igbo villages, reveling in their exoticism, their remoteness, their difference, then swiftly turn around to stress the universality of his characters and situations. But in so doing we lose half its worth. I am not referring to the novel's cultural nationalist politics and its mission to alleviate the psychic injuries of the dispossessed. I am alluding to that elusive quality known as literary value.

Things Fall Apart is, above all, a great work of art. It is incredibly reflective and audacious in its conceptualization, nuanced and complex in its execution, yet—at first appearance—so simple, so unnervingly humble, as to be accessible, on a superficial level, to millions of readers of every age around the world. This accessibility, as we have seen, may have done wonders for Achebe's reputation, but it has also obscured the work's literary quality. It is indeed an entry point into complex African realities, and it does write back to empire. But it is more. As Achebe himself once said, quoting Theodore Roosevelt, "I speak softly, but I carry a big stick."[1] The proverbial big stick is, in many ways, Achebe's legendary ability to speak truth to power and to do so beautifully. But there is more to resistance and contestation than theorization, intertextuality, elaborate realism, and quasi-documentary representation. The formal genius of *Things Fall Apart* lies in the seamless blending of its redefinition of language, its *elasticizing* of the novelistic genre and the invisible presence of his mbari poetics into a work of artistic beauty. And beauty—in and of itself—has a crucial role to play in our politically charged present.

Things Fall Apart has become the stuff of legend, and the academic esteem of *Things Fall Apart* will only increase in the future. Even *Arrow of God,* which most critics—and the author himself—consider a far superior work, is not set to supersede Achebe's first novel any time soon. There is far more to *Things Fall Apart*'s perpetuity than the author's prestige, its cultural nationalist message, or its place in collective memory. It is the recognition, unburdened by academic labels and postcolonial finesse, of the sheer power of its words.

In Africa, *Things Fall Apart* will always hold a place in the heart of the reading public. In the continent and all over the world, it will continue to be a set text in school and university courses. In English-speaking countries, lay readers—responding to reviews, book club requirements, and word-of mouth-endorsements or simply looking to broaden their worldview—will continue to turn to it. What seems less clear is the novel's popular dissemination in non-African and non-Anglophone parts of the world, where its mediation hinges on questions of translational prowess, editorial allure, cultural visibility, the extent of institutional engagement with the imperial past, and many other so-ciocultural variables.

Still, *Things Fall Apart* will remain. But to do so with even more grandeur, it may need to be clad in a different garb. Beyond the hallowed walls of academia, its mode of diffusion may need to change to answer its renewed call. Speaking in another context, Harvard Professor Henry Louis Gates Jr. has asserted that "far too often in the culture wars, we threw the baby out with the bath, and that's not something that we do in our department and not something that our students are allowed to do."[2] Reductive, ethnographic, overcontextualized ways of teaching and promoting translations of *Things Fall Apart* reify difference, in the worst sense of the term, repackage African realities for the neocolonial gaze, feed into an unhealthy obsession with literary and curricular tokenism, and in effect objectify the African novel, thus diminishing its artistic achievements.

"*Things Fall Apart* will survive its ideological admirers," Harold Bloom categorically—and somewhat polemically—states. "Its firmly controlled prose, profound compassion and long insight into its people will not wear out."[3] Without belittling the potential of the biographical, historical, and social contexts of the novel in the classroom and in public discussion, the time has come to stretch its possibilities for intercultural communication to the limit by advocating a "formal turn." *Things Fall Apart* is one of the finest literary works of twentieth-century *world* literature. It is a modern classic. To stress this fact to the world is our prerogative at this particular time in history. When we speak, let us speak for art, and let art speak for itself.

Notes

Introduction

1. S. Gikandi, *Reading Chinua Achebe: Language and Ideology in Fiction* (Oxford: James Currey, 1991), 79.

2. E. Boehmer, "Achebe and His Influence in Some Contemporary African Writing," *Interventions: Journal of Postcolonial Studies* 11, no. 2 (2009): 148.

Chapter 1: The World of Stories

1. C. Achebe, "Named for Victoria, Queen of England," in *Hopes and Impediments: Selected Essays* (New York: Anchor Books, 1990), 37–38.

2. C. Achebe, *There Was a Country: A Personal History of Biafra* (New York: Penguin Books, 2012), 15. Umejiofo Achebe (not related), for that was the supposed madman's name, had been a schoolteacher before his insanity became apparent. See Ezenwa-Ohaeto, *Chinua Achebe: A Biography* (Oxford: James Currey, 1997), 17.

3. Achebe, *There Was a Country,* 18.

4. The singular of of *ndioka* is *onyeoka*.

5. Professor Cole read a draft of this chapter and made some helpful suggestions. It is to his work that I will turn as I draw out connections between mbari and Achebe's work.

6. C. Achebe, "The Igbo World and Its Art," in *Hopes and Impediments,* 64–65.

7. A. Kalu, "African Literature and the Traditional Arts: Speaking Art, Molding Theory," *Research in African Literatures* 31, no. 1 (2000): 48–62.

8. H. M. Cole, *Mbari: Art and Life among the Owerri Igbo* (Bloomington: Indiana University Press, 1982), 219.

9. S. O. Ogbechie, "The Historical Life of Objects: Art History and the Problem of Discourse Obsolescence," *African Arts* 38, no. 4 (2005): 66.

10. Cole, *Mbari,* 216.

11. H. M. Cole, "The Survival and Impact of Igbo Mbari," *African Arts* 21, no. 1 (1988): 62.

12. Chinua Achebe, "The Novelist as Teacher," in *Hopes and Impediments,* 45.

13. Cole, *Mbari,* 159.

14. Ibid., 164.

15. G. R. Carpio, *Laughing Fit to Kill: Black Humor in the Fictions of Slavery* (New York: Oxford University Press, 2008), 11.

16. Cole, *Mbari,* 207.

Chapter 2: Encounters with the Colonial Library

1. C. Achebe, "The Education of a British-Protected Child," *Cambridge Review* 114 (1993): 56.

2. See T. Ochiagha, *Achebe and Friends at Umuahia: The Making of a Literary Elite* (Oxford: James Currey, 2015); and T. Ochiagha, "There Was a College: Introducing *The Umuahian: A Golden Jubilee Publication,*" *Africa: Journal of the International Africa Institute* 85, no. 2 (2015): 191–220.

3. C. Achebe, "African Literature as Restoration of Celebration," in *Chinua Achebe: A Celebration,* ed. K. H. Petersen and A. Rutherford (Oxford: Heinemann Educational Books, 1991), 7.

4. C. Achebe, "My Home under Imperial Fire," in *Home and Exile* (Edinburgh: Canongate, 2003), 21.

5. He initially enrolled in geography instead of religion, but switched when he discovered Geoffrey Parrinder's course on comparative West African religions.

6. Quoted in R. Wren, *Those Magical Years: The Making of Nigerian Literature at Ibadan, 1948–1966* (Washington, DC: Three Continents, 1991), 91.

7. C. Achebe, "Named for Victoria, Queen of England," in *Hopes and Impediments: Selected Essays* (New York: Anchor Books, 1990), 30–40.

8. Ezenwa-Ohaeto, *Chinua Achebe: A Biography* (Oxford: James Currey, 1997).

9. Quoted in ibid., 43.

10. B. Lindfors, *Early Nigerian Literature* (New York: Africana, 1982), 98.

Chapter 3: The Lost Manuscript and Other Harrowing Adventures

1. C. Achebe, "The Empire Fights Back," in *Home and Exile* (Edinburgh: Canongate, 2003), 38.

2. C. Achebe, "The Novelist as Teacher," in *Hopes and Impediments: Selected Essays* (New York: Anchor Books, 1990), 45.

3. C. Achebe, *There Was a Country: A Personal History of Biafra* (New York: Penguin Books, 2012), 34. 4.

Achebe, "Novelist as Teacher," 43.

5. Ibid., 44.

6. Achebe, *There Was a Country,* 35.

7. Ibid., 39.8.

8. C. Clarke, "Uche Okeke and Chinua Achebe: Artist and Author in Conversation," *Critical Interventions: Journal of African Art History and Visual Culture* 1 (2007): 146–47.

9. Achebe, *There Was a Country,* 33.

10. D. C. Moore, A. Heath, and C. Achebe, "A Conversation with Chinua Achebe," *Transition,* no. 100 (2008): 30.

11. Chinua Achebe, quoted in Ezenwa-Ohaeto, *Chinua Achebe: A Biography* (Oxford: James Currey, 1997), 62.

12. Obi Nwakanma, *Thirsting for Sunlight, 1930–1967* (Oxford: James Currey, 2010), 110.

13. Quoted in J. Currey, *Africa Writes Back: The African Writers Series and the Launch of African Literature* (Oxford: James Currey, 2008), 30.

14. J. Currey, *Africa Writes Back*, 29.

15. Quoted in ibid., 29.

16. Achebe, *There Was a Country*, 37. In sheer contrast to the novel itself, the original manuscript of *Things Fall Apart* seems to have been jinxed. A Cameroonian professor of English in Yaoundé, Paul Meloni, who claimed to be working on a comparative study of Achebe and Yeats, persuaded Achebe to loan him the manuscript for a weekend. As Ernest Emenyonu puts it, he "vanished into thin air," and Achebe's attempts to contact him were unfruitful. E. Emenyonu, "Chinua Achebe and African Literature: Yesterday, Today and Tomorrow," *The Source*, April 8, 2013, http://www.thesourceng.com/Today-April82013.htm.

When Meloni died, Achebe made a further attempt to retrieve the manuscript, but Meloni's brother, a lawyer, claimed to have searched in vain for it among his possessions. R. U. Mezu, *Chinua Achebe: The Man and His Works* (London: Adonis and Abbey, 2006), 246.

The manuscript remains lost, although Cameroonian scholar Joyce Ashuntantang has been trying, without success, to bring its story to a happy end. J. Ashuntantang, "50 Years after 'Things Fall Apart': A Chat with Chinua Achebe," *Scribbles from the Den* (blog), February 21, 2008, http://www.dibussi.com/2008/02/50-years-after.html.

17. Achebe, *There Was a Country*, 38.

18. Ibid.

19. Alan Hill, quoted in Currey, *Africa Writes Back*, 65.

Chapter 4: A Literary Revolution

1. D. C. Moore, A. Heath, and C. Achebe, "A Conversation with Chinua Achebe," *Transition*, no. 100 (2008): 30.

2. This, of course, was a hackneyed judgment that Achebe himself did not share. See his "Work and Play in Tutuola's *The Palm-Wine Drinkard*," in *Hopes and Impediments: Selected Essays* (New York: Anchor Books), 100–113.

3. Ezenwa-Ohaeto, *Chinua Achebe: A Biography* (Oxford: James Currey, 1997), 68.

4. G. Adali-Mortty, review of *Things Fall Apart,* by Chinua Achebe, *Black Orpheus,* no. 6 (1959): 50.

5. Moore, Heath, and Achebe, "A Conversation with Chinua Achebe," 30.

6. S. Rodman, "The White Man's Faith: Things Fall Apart by Chinua Achebe," *New York Times,* February 22, 1959; V. Yudkin, review of *Things Fall Apart, Washington Post,* February 22, 1959, quoted in M. E. Oliver, "Humble Beginnings of Chinua Achebe's 'Things Fall Apart,'" *Washington Post,* March 22, 2013, https://www.washingtonpost.com/news/arts-and-entertainment/wp/2013/03/22/humble-beginnings-of-chinua-achebes-things-fall-apart/?utm_term=.6e60fd4d64c0; R. C. Healy, review of *Things Fall Apart, New York Herald Tribune,* April 12, 1959, 8.

7. Elechi Amadi, for instance, had actually set a short story in a precolonial village milieu during his Umuahia school days, inspired by the endless narratives of a village raconteur. See T. Ochiagha, *Achebe and Friends at Umuahia: The Making of a Literary Elite* (Oxford: James Currey, 2015), 114.

8. Quoted in R. Wren, *Those Magical Years: The Making of Nigerian Literature at Ibadan, 1948-1966* (Washington, DC: Three Continents, 1991), 71.

9. The majority of Nigeria's first-generation writers were Igbos, but the observation still holds for the literary transposition of other Nigerian languages into English.

10. S. Gikandi, "Chinua Achebe and the Invention of African Literature," in C. Achebe, *Things Fall Apart* (Oxford: Heinemann, 1996), xvii.

11. I. Bello-Kano, "Chinua Achebe: A Dissenting Opinion," in *Chinua Achebe: Tributes and Reflections,* ed. N. A. Clarke and J. Currey (Branford: Ayebia Clarke, 2014), 113.

12. S. Newell, *West African Literature: Ways of Reading* (Oxford: Oxford University Press, 2006), 98.

13. A. F. Irele, "Chinua Achebe (1930–2013): A Summing Up," in Clarke and Currey, *Chinua Achebe: Tributes and Reflections,* 59.

1. A. Mukherjee, *What Is a Classic? Postcolonial Rewriting and Invention of the Canon* (Stanford: Stanford University Press, 2013), 96.

2. See S. Newell, *West African Literature: Ways of Reading* (Oxford: Oxford University Press, 2006), 97; G. Huggan, *The Postcolonial Exotic: Marketing the Margins* (London: Routledge, 2001), 39.

3. S. D. Hassan, "Canons after Postcolonial Studies," *Pedagogy: Critical Approaches to Teaching Literature, Language, Composition and Culture* 1 (2001): 2.

4. C. Achebe, "An Image of Africa: Racism in Conrad's Heart of Darkness," in *Hopes and Impediments: Selected Essays* (New York: Anchor Books, 1990), 1–20; O. Okunoye, "Half a Century of Reading Chinua Achebe's *Things Fall Apart*," *English Studies* 91, no. 1 (2010): 55.

5. S. Gikandi, *Reading Chinua Achebe: Language and Ideology in Fiction* (Oxford: James Currey, 1991), 26.

6. A. JanMohamed, "Sophisticated Primitivism: The Syncretism of Oral and Literature Modes in Achebe's *Things Fall Apart*," *Ariel: A Review of International African Literature* 15, no. 4 (1984): 38.

7. B. Jeyifo, "For Chinua Achebe: The Resilience and the Predicament of Obierika," in *Chinua Achebe: A Celebration*, ed. K. H. Petersen and A. Rutherford (Oxford: Heinemann, 1990), 51–70.

8. A. Quayson, "Realism, Criticism and the Disguises of Both: A Reading of Chinua Achebe's *Things Fall Apart* with an Evaluation of the Criticism Relating to It," *Research in African Literatures* 25, no. 4 (1994): 118.

9. F. Stratton, *Contemporary African Literature and the Politics of Gender* (London: Routledge, 1994).

10. B. Jeyifo, "Okonkwo and His Mother: Things Fall Apart and Issues of Gender in the Constitution of African Postcolonial Discourse," in *Chinua Achebe's* Things Fall Apart: *A Case Book*, ed. I. Okpewho (Oxford: Oxford University Press, 2003), 183.

11. Gikandi, *Reading Chinua Achebe,* 47–48.

12. Quayson, "Realism, Criticism," 129.

13. N. Achebe, "Balancing the Male and Female Principles: Teaching about Gender in Chinua Achebe's *Things Fall Apart,*" *Ufahamu: A Journal of African Studies* 29, no. 1 (2002): 122.

14. Ibid., 139.

Chapter 6: Of Canons, Sons, and Daughters

1. According to James Currey, "when William Heinemann published hardbacks of *Things Fall Apart* in 1958, and its sequel *No Longer at Ease* in 1960, hardly anybody knew about Achebe's achievement in his own country, Nigeria. The appointment in 1962 of Chinua Achebe as Editorial Adviser to the Series did mean that many of the early titles were from Nigeria. His example had set a trend and it was in Nigeria that the novel first took off in Africa." J. Currey, *Africa Writes Back: The African Writers Series and the Launch of African Literature* (Oxford: James Currey, 2008), 39. However, word-of-mouth diffusion accounts for the like-minded friends and acquaintances among Nigeria's first-generation writers.

2. A. A. Aidoo, "Remembering Chinua Achebe," in *Chinua Achebe: Tributes and Reflections,* ed. N. A. Clarke and J. Currey (Branford: Ayebia Clarke, 2014), 69.

3. C. Achebe, "Politics and Politicians of Language in African Literature," in *The Education of a British-Protected Child* (New York: Alfred A. Knopf, 2009), 97–99.

4. N. Thiong'o, "Chinua Achebe: The Spirit Lives," in Clarke and Currey, *Chinua Achebe: Tributes and Reflections,* 40.

5. In response to a question on whether she thought that Nigerian fiction was largely imitative of Achebe, Molly Mahood, a critic who had been a professor and head of English at University College, Ibadan, responded, "the worst writers, the poorer writers have, of course, thought that he was simply writing fictionalized anthropology and they've produced anthropology which wasn't even very well fictionalized. But I would have thought that the better writers were quite clear about what they wanted to do." In R. Wren, *Those Magical*

Years: The Making of Nigerian Literature at Ibadan, 1948–1966 (Washington, DC: Three Continents, 1991), 27.

6. Currey, *Africa Writes Back,* 52.

7. Ibid., 48.

8. Ibid., 53.

9. Ibid.

10. A. P. Busia, "A Poet Daughter's Farewell: Still Morning Yet," in Clarke and Currey, *Chinua Achebe: Tributes and Reflections,* 125–26.

11. C. A. Adichie, "Chinua Achebe at 82: We Remember Differently," in Clarke and Currey, *Chinua Achebe: Tributes and Reflections,* 90.

12. Ibid.

13. E. Eisenberg, "'Real Africa'/'Which Africa?': The Critique of Mimetic Realism in Chimamanda Adichie's Short Fiction," in *Writing Africa in the Short Story,* ed. E. Emenyonu (Oxford: James Currey, 2013), 21.

14. B. Doherty, "Writing Back with a Difference: Chimamanda Ngozi Adichie's 'The Headstrong Historian' as a Response to Chinua Achebe's *Things Fall Apart,*" in *Tradition and Change in Contemporary West and East African Fiction,* ed. O. Okuyade (Amsterdam: Rodopi, 2014), 188.

15. Boehmer, "Achebe and His Influence," 143.

16. Ibid., 152.

17. Quoted in H. Habila, "An Interview with Chinua Achebe," in Clarke and Currey, *Chinua Achebe: Tributes and Reflections,* 167.

Chapter 7: Artistic Interactions

1. D. C. Moore, A. Heath, and C. Achebe, "A Conversation with Chinua Achebe," *Transition,* no. 100 (2008): 13.

2. Ibid.

3. See all the covers in ibid.

4. Quoted in ibid., 21.

5. For all the illustrations of *Things Fall Apart,* see E. Hyde, "Flat Style: *Things Fall Apart* and Its Illustrations," *PMLA* 131, no. 1 (2016): 20–37.

6. Ibid., 27.

7. C. Okeke-Agulu, "The Politics of Form: Uche Okeke's Illustrations for Achebe's *Things Fall Apart,*" in *Chinua Achebe's* Things Fall Apart, *1958–2008,* ed. D. Whittaker (Amsterdam: Rodopi, 2011), 72.

8. C. Clarke, "Uche Okeke and Chinua Achebe: Artist and Author in Conversation," *Critical Interventions: Journal of African Art History and Visual Culture* 1, no. 11 (2007): 148.

9. Okeke-Agulu, "The Politics of Form," 68.

10. Ibid., 75.

11. Hyde, "Flat Style," 29.

12. Okeke-Agulu, "The Politics of Form," 72.

13. Ibid., 84–85.

14. C. Okeke-Agulu, *Postcolonial Modernism: Art and Decolonization in Twentieth-Century Nigeria* (Durham, NC: Duke University Press, 2015), 273–74. A reproduction of the painting appears on page 273.

15. Moore, Heath, and Achebe, "A Conversation with Chinua Achebe," 24, 26.

16. G. Huggan, *The Postcolonial Exotic: Marketing the Margins* (London: Routledge, 2001), 53–54.

17. Moore, Heath, and Achebe, "A Conversation with Chinua Achebe," 29.

18. Ibid., 32.

19. See Pitts Rivers Museum, 1972.24.67: face and head mask, accessed November 26, 2017, http://objects.prm.ox.ac .uk/pages/PRMUID116074.html.

Chapter 8: Adaptations, Appropriations, and Mimesis

1. M. K. Booker, "Bullfrog in the Sun," in *The Chinua Achebe Encyclopedia,* ed. M. K. Booker (Westport, CT: Greenwood, 2003), 49.

2. Quoted in H. Ekwuazi, "Political Values and the Nigerian Film," in *No Condition Is Permanent: Nigerian Writing and the Struggle for Democracy,* ed. H. Ehlin and C.-P. Holste–von Mutius (Amsterdam: Rodopi, 2001), 280.

3. F. Ugochukwu, "Things Fall Apart—Achebe's Legacy, from Book to Screen," *Research in African Literatures* 45, no. 2 (2014): 169.

4. D. C. Moore, A. Heath, and C. Achebe, "A Conversation with Chinua Achebe," *Transition,* no. 100 (2008): 24.

5. T. Ochiagha, "Decolonizing the Mind Onitsha-Style: Re-examining Ogali A. Ogali's Cultural Nationalism in *The Juju Priest,*" *Research in African Literatures* 46, no. 1 (2015): 102.

6. Ezenwa-Ohaeto, *Chinua Achebe: A Biography* (Oxford: James Currey, 1997), 246.

7. The series was aired again after 1986. I recall watching it sometime in the second half of 1988 as a child in Nigeria. Recently, Mediafric TV, London, has uploaded the series on YouTube "in voluntary contribution to African history." Coinciding with the fiftieth anniversary of *Things Fall Apart,* it was reissued by a Nigerian production company. See Ugochukwu, "Things Fall Apart," 170.

8. Ibid.

9. Ibid., 176.

10. C. Eke, "'Things Fall Apart and I': Pete Edochie, a Popular Nigerian Actor and a Foremost Broadcaster," *Naijarules:* Forums, November 14, 2008, https://www.naijarules.com/index .php? threads/things-fall-apart-and-i-pete-edochie.30790/.

11. Ibid.

12. Ugochukwu, "Things Fall Apart," 172.

13. Ibid., 173.

14. Ibid., 179.

15. B. Njoku, "How Pete Edochie was Chosen for Things Fall Apart," *Vanguard,* June 20, 2015, https://www.vanguardngr .com/2015/06/how-pete-edochie-was-chosen-for-things-fall -apart/.

16. "*Things Fall Apart*—Theatre Performance," accessed November 29, 2017, https://www.youtube.com/watch? v =suK1YMlHN58.

17. R. H. Cataliotti, *The Songs Became the Stories: The Musician in African-American Fiction, 1970–2005* (Oxford: Peter Lang, 2007), 74.

18. C. Ryan, "The Roots: Things Fall Apart (MCA, 1998)," in *Classical Material: The Hip-Hop Album Guide,* ed. Oliver Wang (Toronto: ECW Press, 2003), 142.

19. J. B. Peterson, *The Hip-Hop Underground and African American Culture: Beneath the Surface* (New York: Palgrave Macmillan, 2014).

20. A. Thompson and B. Greenman, *Mo' Meta Blues: The World According to Quest* (New York: Grand Central, 2013).

21. R. Dryden, "Art Director Kenny Gravillis Tells the Stories behind The Roots' 5 'Things Fall Apart' Album Covers," Complex, February 23, 2014, www.complex.com/style/2014/02/the-roots-things-fall-apart-album-covers/.

22. S. Michaels, "Chinua Achebe Forces 50 Cent to Rename Movie," *Guardian* (US), September 14, 2011, https://www.theguardian.com/music/2011/sep/14/chinua-achebe-50-cent.

23. The misspelling is not accidental. See E. Effiong, "The Storyteller's Review of Chude Jideonwo's Review of Anakle's 'Things Come Together' Ad for Wikipedia," *Guardian* (Nigeria), October 23, 2017, https://guardian.ng/art/the-storytellers-review-of-chude-jideonwos-review-of-anakles-things-come-together-ad-for-wikipedia/.

24. I am indebted to my colleague, the historian Anna Maguire of King's College, London, for this observation.

25. "Things Come Together with Pete Edochie," accessed November 29, 2017, https://twitter.com/Wikipedia/status/912564155118272512?ref_src=twsrc%5Etfw&ref_url=https%3A%2F%2Fwww.pulse.ng%2Fentertainment%2Fmovies%2Fpete-edochie-is-okonkwo-in-new-skit-things-fall-together-id7376607.html.

Chapter 9: *Things Fall Apart*'s Worldwide Readers

1. K. A. Appiah, *In My Father's House: Africa in the Philosophy of Culture* (New York: Oxford University Press, 1992), 87.

2. C. Achebe, "An Image of Africa: Racism in Conrad's *Heart of Darkness,*" in *Hopes and Impediments: Selected Essays* (New York: Anchor Books, 1990), 2–3.

3. J. Procter, "Reading, Taste and Postcolonial Studies," *Interventions: Journal of Postcolonial Studies* 11, no. 2 (2009): 192.

4. Ibid., 193.

5. Ibid., 183.

6. W. Lubiano, "Narrative, Metacommentary and Politics in a 'Simple' Story," in *Approaches to Teaching Achebe's* Things Fall Apart, ed. B. Lindfors (New York: MLA, 1991), 110.

7. See G. Huggan, *The Postcolonial Exotic: Marketing the Margins* (London: Routledge, 2001).

8. R. Bush, "*Le monde s'effondre?* Translating Anglophone African Literature in the World Republic of Letters," *Journal of Postcolonial Writing* 48, no. 5 (2016): 522.

9. Ibid.

10. E. R. Murphy, "Entrevista a Marta Sofía López Rodríguez, traductora de 'No Longer at Ease' y 'Anthills of the Savannah' de Chinua Achebe," *TRANS: Revista de traductología*, no. 18 (2014): 241–50.

11. Bush, "*Le monde s'effondre?*," 522.

12. R. Granqvist, "The Early Swedish Reviews of Chinua Achebe's *Things Fall Apart* and *A Man of the People*," *Research in African Literatures* 15, no. 3 (1984): 394–404.

13. B. Lindfors, preface to Lindfors, *Approaches to Teaching Achebe's* Things Fall Apart, ix.

14. S. Gikandi, "Chinua Achebe and the Signs of the Times," in Lindfors, *Approaches to Teaching Achebe's* Things Fall Apart, 26–27.

15. Lubiano, "Narrative, Metacommentary and Politics," 111.

16. C. Achebe, "Teaching *Things Fall Apart*," in Lindfors, *Approaches to Teaching Achebe's* Things Fall Apart, 20.

Conclusion: Whither *Things Fall Apart*?

1. "Prof. Chinua Achebe Speaking at Harvard," accessed November 18, 2017, https://www.youtube.com/watch? time _continue=4&v=KiLVnN5YNno.

2. Quoted in B. Cole, "Resurrecting the Texts: A Conversation with Henry Louis Gates, Jr.," *Humanities: The Magazine of the National Endowment for the Humanities* 23, no. 2 (2002), https://

www.neh.gov/humanities/2002/marchapril/conversation/resurrecting-the-texts.

3. H. Bloom, "Introduction," in *Chinua Achebe's* Things Fall Apart, Bloom's Modern Critical Interpretations (New York: Chelsea House, 2010), 2.

Bibliography

Selected Editions of *Things Fall Apart*

Things Fall Apart. London: William Heinemann, 1958.

Things Fall Apart. New York: Alfred A. Knopf, 1958.

Things Fall Apart. Greenwich, CT: Fawcett Crest, 1959.

Things Fall Apart. New York: McDowell, Obolensky, 1959.

Things Fall Apart. New York: Astor-Honor, 1959.

Things Fall Apart. London: Heinemann, 1962.

Things Fall Apart. London: Heinemann, 1963.

Things Fall Apart. Greenwich, CT: Fawcett Crest, 1969.

Things Fall Apart. London: Heinemann Educational, 1971.

Things Fall Apart. Adapted by John Davey. London: Heinemann, 1974.

Things Fall Apart. London: Heinemann 1976.

Things Fall Apart. London: Heinemann, 1986.

Things Fall Apart. Introduction by Kwame Anthony Appiah. London: Everyman's Library, 1992.

Things Fall Apart. New York: Doubleday, 1994.

Things Fall Apart. New York: Anchor, 1994.

Things Fall Apart. Expanded edition with notes. London: Heinemann, 1996.

Things Fall Apart and Related Readings. Evanston, IL: McDougal Littell, 1997.

Things Fall Apart: With Connections. New York: Holt Rinehart and Winston, 1999.

Things Fall Apart. Introduction by Biyi Bandele-Thomas. Harmondsworth: Penguin, 2001.

Things Fall Apart. Nairobi: East African Educational Publishers, 2001.

Things Fall Apart: With Related Readings. St Paul: EMC/Paradigm Publishing, 2002.

Things Fall Apart. Fiftieth Anniversary Edition. New York: Anchor, 2008.

Things Fall Apart. Oxford: Heinemann, 2008.

Things Fall Apart. London: The Folio Society, 2008.

Things Fall Apart. Norton Critical Edition, edited by Abiola Francis Irele. New York: W. W. Norton, 2009.

The African Trilogy: Things Fall Apart, No Longer at Ease, Arrow of God. London: Everyman, 2011.

The African Trilogy. Foreword by Kwame Anthony Appiah. London: Penguin, 2017.

Things Fall Apart. London: Penguin, 2018.

Selected Translations Discussed in This Book

Achebe, C. *Le monde s'effondre*. Translated by Michel Ligny. Paris: Présence Africaine, 1966.

———. *Allt gar sönder*. Translated by Ebbe Linde. Stockholm: Albert Bonniers, 1967.

———. *Todo se desmorona*. Translated by Marta Sofía López Rodríguez. Barcelona: Random House Mondadori, 2010.

Other Works Cited

Achebe, C. "African Literature as Restoration of Celebration." In Petersen and Rutherford, *Chinua Achebe: A Celebration*, 1–10.

———. "The Education of a British-Protected Child." *Cambridge Review* 114 (1993): 51–57.

———. "The Empire Fights Back." In Achebe, *Home and Exile*, 37–73.

———. *Home and Exile*. Edinburgh: Canongate, 2003.

———. *Hopes and Impediments: Selected Essays*. New York: Anchor Books, 1990.

———. "The Igbo World and Its Art." In Achebe, *Hopes and Impediments*, 62–68.

————. "An Image of Africa: Racism in Conrad's *Heart of Darkness*." In Achebe, *Hopes and Impediments*, 1–20.

————. "My Home under Imperial Fire." In Achebe, *Home and Exile*, 1–37.

————. "Named for Victoria, Queen of England." In Achebe, *Hopes and Impediments*, 30–40.

————. "The Novelist as Teacher." In Achebe, *Hopes and Impediments*, 45.

————. "Politics and Politicians of Language in African Literature." In *The Education of a British-Protected Child*, 97–99. New York: Alfred A. Knopf, 2009.

————. "Teaching *Things Fall Apart*." In Lindfors, *Approaches to Teaching Achebe's* Things Fall Apart, 20–25.

————. *There Was a Country: A Personal History of Biafra.* New York: Penguin Books, 2012.

————. "Work and Play in Tutuola's *The Palm-Wine Drinkard*." In Achebe, *Hopes and Impediments*, 100–113.

Achebe, N. "Balancing the Male and Female Principles: Teaching about Gender in Chinua Achebe's *Things Fall Apart*." *Ufahamu: A Journal of African Studies* 29, no. 1 (2002): 121–43.

Adali-Mortty, G. Review of *Things Fall Apart*, by Chinua Achebe. *Black Orpheus*, no. 6 (1959): 48–50.

Adichie, C. A. "Chinua Achebe at 82: We Remember Differently." In Clarke and Currey, *Chinua Achebe: Tributes and Reflections*, 90–98.

Aidoo, A. A. "Remembering Chinua Achebe." In Clarke and Currey, *Chinua Achebe: Tributes and Reflections*, 67–71.

Appiah, K. A. *In My Father's House: Africa in the Philosophy of Culture.* New York: Oxford University Press, 1992.

Ashuntantang, J. "50 Years After 'Things Fall Apart': A Chat with Chinua Achebe." *Scribbles from the Den* (blog), February 21, 2008. http://www.dibussi.com/2008/02/50 -years-after.html.

Bello-Kano, I. "Chinua Achebe: A Dissenting Opinion." In Clarke and Currey, *Chinua Achebe: Tributes and Reflections*, 112–19.

Bloom, H. "Introduction." In *Chinua Achebe's* Things Fall Apart, 1–5. Bloom's Modern Critical Interpretations. New York: Chelsea House, 2010.

Boehmer, E. "Achebe and His Influence in Some Contemporary African Writing." *Interventions: Journal of Postcolonial Studies* 11, no. 2 (2009): 141–53.

Booker, M. K. "Bullfrog in the Sun." In *The Chinua Achebe Encyclopedia,* edited by M. K. Booker, 49–50. Westport, CT: Greenwood, 2003.

Bush, R. "*Le monde s'effondre?* Translating Anglophone African Literature in the World Republic of Letters." *Journal of Postcolonial Writing* 48, no. 5 (2016): 512–25.

Busia, A. P. "A Poet Daughter's Farewell: Still Morning Yet." In Clarke and Currey, *Chinua Achebe: Tributes and Reflections,* 125–26.

Carpio, G. R. *Laughing Fit to Kill: Black Humor in the Fictions of Slavery.* New York: Oxford University Press, 2008.

Cataliotti, R. H. *The Songs Became the Stories: The Musician in African-American Fiction, 1970–2005.* Oxford: Peter Lang, 2007.

Clarke, C. "Uche Okeke and Chinua Achebe: Artist and Author in Conversation." *Critical Interventions: Journal of African Art History and Visual Culture* 1 (2007): 143–53.

Clarke, N. A., and J. Currey, eds. *Chinua Achebe: Tributes and Reflections.* Branford: Ayebia Clarke, 2014.

Cole, B. "Resurrecting the Texts: A Conversation with Henry Louis Gates, Jr." *Humanities: The Magazine of the National Endowment for the Humanities* 23, no. 2 (2002). https://www.neh.gov/humanities/2002/marchapril/conversation/resurrecting-the-texts.

Cole, H. M. *Mbari: Art and Life among the Owerri Igbo.* Bloomington: Indiana University Press, 1982.

———. "The Survival and Impact of Igbo Mbari." *African Arts* 21, no. 1 (1988): 54–96.

Currey, J. *Africa Writes Back: The African Writers Series and the Launch of African Literature.* Oxford: James Currey, 2008.

Doherty, B. "Writing Back with a Difference: Chimamanda Ngozi Adichie's 'The Headstrong Historian' as a Response to Chinua Achebe's *Things Fall Apart*." In *Tradition and Change in Contemporary West and East African Fiction,* edited by O. Okuyade, 187–203. Amsterdam: Rodopi, 2014.

Dryden, R. "Art Director Kenny Gravillis Tells the Stories behind The Roots' 5 'Things Fall Apart' Album Covers." *Complex,* February 23, 2014. www.complex.com/style /2014/02/the-roots-things-fall-apart-album-covers/.

Effiong, E. "The Storyteller's Review of Chude Jideonwo's Review of Anakle's 'Things Come Together' Ad for Wikipedia." *Guardian* (Nigeria), October 23, 2017. https:// guardian.ng/art/the-storytellers-review-of-chude -jideonwos-review-of-anakles-things-come-together -ad-for-wikipedia/.

Eisenberg, E. "'Real Africa'/'Which Africa?': The Critique of Mimetic Realism in Chimamanda Ngozi Adichie's Short Fiction." In *Writing Africa in the Short Story,* edited by E. N. Emenyonu, 8–25. Oxford: James Currey, 2013.

Eke, C. "'Things Fall Apart and I': Pete Edochie, a Popular Nigerian Actor and a Foremost Broadcaster." *Naijarules:* Forums, November 14, 2008. Accessed November 29, 2017. https://www.naijarules.com/index.php?threads/things -fall-apart-and-i-pete-edochie.30790/.

Ekwuazi, H. "Political Values and the Nigerian Film." In *No Condition Is Permanent: Nigerian Writing and the Struggle for Democracy,* edited by H. Ehlin and C.-P. Holste–von Mutius, 275–80. Amsterdam: Rodopi, 2001.

Emenyonu, E. "Chinua Achebe and African Literature: Yesterday, Today and Tomorrow." *The Source,* April 8, 2013. http://www.thesourceng.com/TodayApril82013.htm.

Ezenwa-Ohaeto. *Chinua Achebe: A Biography.* Oxford: James Currey, 1997.

Gikandi, S. "Chinua Achebe and the Invention of African Literature." In C. Achebe, *Things Fall Apart,* xvii. Oxford: Heinemann, 1996.

————. "Chinua Achebe and the Signs of the Times." In Lindfors, *Approaches to Teaching Achebe's* Things Fall Apart, 25–31.

————. *Reading Chinua Achebe: Language and Ideology in Fiction.* Oxford: James Currey, 1991.

Granqvist, R. "The Early Swedish Reviews of Chinua Achebe's *Things Fall Apart* and *A Man of the People.*" *Research in African Literatures* 15, no. 3 (1984): 394–404.

Habila, H. "An Interview with Chinua Achebe." In Clarke and Currey, *Chinua Achebe: Tributes and Reflections,* 165–67.

Hassan, S. D. "Canons after Postcolonial Studies." *Pedagogy: Critical Approaches to Teaching Literature, Language, Composition and Culture* 1, no. 2 (2001).

Healy, R. C. Review of *Things Fall Apart. New York Herald Tribune,* April 12, 1959, 8.

Huggan, G. *The Postcolonial Exotic: Marketing the Margins.* London: Routledge, 2001.

Hyde, E. "Flat Style: *Things Fall Apart* and Its Illustrations." *PMLA* 131, no. 1 (2016): 20–37.

Irele, A. F. "Chinua Achebe (1930–2013): A Summing Up." In Clarke and Currey, *Chinua Achebe: Tributes and Reflections,* 58–67.

JanMohamed, A. "Sophisticated Primitivism: The Syncretism of Oral and Literature Modes in Achebe's *Things Fall Apart.*" *Ariel: A Review of International African Literature* 15, no. 4 (1984): 19–39.

Jeyifo, B. "For Chinua Achebe: The Resilience and the Predicament of Obierika." In Petersen and Rutherford, *Chinua Achebe: A Celebration,* 51–70.

————. "Okonkwo and His Mother: *Things Fall Apart* and Issues of Gender in the Constitution of African Postcolonial Discourse." In *Chinua Achebe's* Things Fall Apart: *A Case Book,* edited by I. Okpewho, 181–200. Oxford: Oxford University Press, 2003.

Kalu, A. "African Literature and the Traditional Arts: Speaking Art, Molding Theory." *Research in African Literatures* 31, no. 1 (2000): 48–62.

Lindfors, B., ed. *Approaches to Teaching Achebe's* Things Fall Apart. New York: MLA, 1991.

————. *Early Nigerian Literature.* New York: Africana, 1982.

———. Preface to Lindfors, *Approaches to Teaching Achebe's Things Fall Apart*, ix–x.

Lubiano, W. "Narrative, Metacommentary and Politics in a 'Simple' Story." In Lindfors, *Approaches to Teaching Achebe's Things Fall Apart*, 107–10.

Mezu, R. U. *Chinua Achebe: The Man and His Works.* London: Adonis and Abbey, 2006.

Michaels, S. "Chinua Achebe Forces 50 Cent to Rename Movie." *Guardian* (US), September 14, 2011. https://www.theguardian.com/music/2011/sep/14/chinua-achebe-50-cent.

Moore, D. C., A. Heath, and C. Achebe. "A Conversation with Chinua Achebe." *Transition,* no. 100 (2008): 12–33.

Mukherjee, A. *What Is a Classic? Postcolonial Rewriting and Invention of the Canon.* Stanford: Stanford University Press, 2013.

Murphy, E. R. "Entrevista a Marta Sofía López Rodríguez, traductora de 'No Longer at Ease' y 'Anthills of the Savannah' de Chinua Achebe." *TRANS: Revista de traductología,* no. 18 (2014): 241–50.

Newell, S. *West African Literature: Ways of Reading.* Oxford: Oxford University Press, 2006.

Njoku, B. "How Pete Edochie Was Chosen for Things Fall Apart." *Vanguard,* June 20, 2015. https://www.vanguardngr.com/2015/06/how-pete-edochie-was-chosen-for-things-fall-apart/.

Nwakanma, O. *Thirsting for Sunlight, 1930–1967.* Oxford: James Currey, 2010.

Ochiagha, T. *Achebe and Friends at Umuahia: The Making of a Literary Elite.* Oxford: James Currey, 2015.

———. "Decolonizing the Mind Onitsha-Style: Re-examining Ogali A. Ogali's Cultural Nationalism in *The Juju Priest.*" *Research in African Literatures* 46, no. 1 (2015): 90–106.

———. "There Was a College: Introducing *The Umuahian: A Golden Jubilee Publication.*" *Africa: Journal of the International Africa Institute* 85, no. 2 (2015): 191–220.

Ogbechie, S. O. "The Historical Life of Objects: Art History and the Problem of Discourse Obsolescence." *African Arts* 38, no. 4 (2005): 66.

Okeke-Agulu, Chika. "The Politics of Form: Uche Okeke's Illustrations for Achebe's *Things Fall Apart*." In *Chinua Achebe's* Things Fall Apart, *1958–2008,* edited by D. Whittaker, 67–89. Amsterdam: Rodopi, 2011.

———. *Postcolonial Modernism: Art and Decolonization in Twentieth-Century Nigeria.* Durham, NC: Duke University Press, 2015.

Okunoye, O. "Half a Century of Reading Chinua Achebe's *Things Fall Apart*." *English Studies* 91, no. 1 (2010): 42–57.

Oliver, M. E. "Humble Beginnings of Chinua Achebe's 'Things Fall Apart.'" *Washington Post,* March 22, 2013. https://www.washingtonpost.com/news/arts-and-entertainment/wp/2013/03/22/humble-beginnings-of-chinua-achebes-things-fall-apart/?utm_term=.6e60fd4d64c0.

Petersen, K. H., and A. Rutherford, eds. *Chinua Achebe: A Celebration.* Oxford: Heinemann, 1990.

Peterson, J. B. *The Hip-Hop Underground and African American Culture: Beneath the Surface.* New York: Palgrave Macmillan, 2014.

Pitts Rivers Museum. "1972.24.67: Face and Head Mask." Accessed November 26, 2017. http://objects.prm.ox.ac.uk/pages/PRMUID116074.html.

Procter, J. "Reading, Taste and Postcolonial Studies." *Interventions: Journal of Postcolonial Studies* 11, no. 2 (2009): 180–98.

"Prof. Chinua Achebe Speaking at Harvard." Accessed November 18, 2017. https://www.youtube.com/watch?time_continue=4&v=KiLVnN5YNno.

Quayson, A. "Realism, Criticism and the Disguises of Both: A Reading of Chinua Achebe's *Things Fall Apart* with an Evaluation of the Criticism Relating to It." *Research in African Literatures* 25, no. 4 (1994): 117–36.

Rodman, S. "The White Man's Faith: Things Fall Apart by Chinua Achebe." *New York Times,* February 22, 1959.

Ryan, C. "The Roots: Things Fall Apart (MCA, 1998)." In *Classical Material: The Hip-Hop Album Guide,* edited by O. Wang, 142. Toronto: ECW Press, 2003.

Stratton, F. *Contemporary African Literature and the Politics of Gender*. London: Routledge, 1994.

"Things Come Together with Pete Edochie." Accessed November 29, 2011. https://twitter.com/Wikipedia/status /912564155118272512? ref_src=twsrc% 5Etfw&ref_url =https% 3A% 2F% 2Fwww.pulse.ng% 2Fentertainment % 2Fmovies% 2Fpete-edochie-is-okonkwo-in-new-skit -things-fall-together-id7376607.html.

"*Things Fall Apart*—Theatre Performance." Accessed November 29, 2017. https://www.youtube.com/watch? v =suK1YMlHN58.

Thiong'o, N. "Chinua Achebe: The Spirit Lives." In Clarke and Currey, *Chinua Achebe: Tributes and Reflections,* 40–45.

Thompson, A., and B. Greenman. *Mo' Meta Blues: The World According to Quest*. New York: Grand Central, 2013.

Ugochukwu, F. "Things Fall Apart—Achebe's Legacy, from Book to Screen." *Research in African Literatures* 45, no. 2 (2014): 168–83.

Wren, R. *Those Magical Years: The Making of Nigerian Literature at Ibadan, 1948–1966*. Washington, D.C.: Three Continents, 1991.

Index

144

145